FOOD FOR FRIENDS

FOOD FOR FRIENDS

SIMPLY DELICIOUS MENUS FOR EASY ENTERTAINING

FRAN WARDE

PHOTOGRAPHY BY Debi Treloar

RYLAND
PETERS
& SMALL

LONDON NEW YORK

First published in Great Britain in 2002
by Ryland Peters & Small
20–21 Jockey's Fields
London WC1R 4BW
www.rylandpeters.com

This paperback edition first published in 2005

10 9 8 7 6 5 4 3 2

Printed and bound in China

ISBN 1 84172 827 6

Senior Designer
Paul Tilby

Editors
Elsa Petersen-Schepelern
Sally Somers

Location Research
Kate Brunt
Sarah Hepworth

Production
Patricia Harrington

Art Director
Gabriella Le Grazie

Publishing Director
Alison Starling

Food Stylist
Fran Warde

Props Stylist
Emily Chalmers

Indexer
Hilary Bird

Dedication

To my Boys, big and little

NOTES
All spoon measurements are level unless
specified otherwise.
Ovens should be preheated to the specified
temperature.
If using a fan-assisted oven, cooking times
should be reduced according to the
manufacturer's instructions.
Specialist Asian ingredients are available in
larger supermarkets and Asian stores.

contents

secrets of easy entertaining

Food and friends go hand in hand, but how many times have we had people coming over for a meal and panicked that we don't know what to make. It doesn't matter how good a cook you are, we all need some inspiration from time to time. When cooking for friends, remember the most important thing is that they came over to talk to you, not to test your cooking skills. Keep it simple, get organized and everything will go smoothly. Choose recipes you know you can manage in your kitchen, with ingredients you know you can find. Read the recipes through before you start, refer to the work plan, then just relax and enjoy the shopping and cooking.

Simplicity is important. Many people have just a handful of recipes they like to cook but if those dishes work and are a pleasure to eat, then no one will mind being served the same thing on more than one occasion.

Don't be afraid to cheat in your kitchen. If you are short of time or energy, buy olives and thinly sliced Parma ham or salami from a good delicatessen. Serve them with some crusty bread and good olive oil, and everyone will be happy. Then you just have to cook one course – the main or pudding – and buy the other. You can find delicious fruit tarts from pâtisseries, hand-made meat pies from good butchers and stuffed pastas and sauces from Italian stores. Don't be ashamed to buy some of the food – good cooking starts with the shopping!

Shop and cook – yes, entertaining is as simple as that.

I like to shop from small traders. Their produce is less likely to be mass-produced and transported unnecessary distances, and will taste better for it, I promise you. It can be more expensive, but it's really worth it, for quality as well as to lend support to small, local producers.

I find that choosing a style is important as it can add a little extra drama and beauty to the meal. You can take it as far as you wish: you'll find it's fun to vary the traditional presentation with everyone sitting around the table with the same food and uniform look. Be bold. This doesn't mean buying a whole new set of china – it's about adding your own touches; napkins tied with herbs, bamboo stalks as flowers, or just petals and candles floating in a large shallow dish. Add glitter to the flower water, put pebbles on the table to create that seaside look, use shells for individual salt and peppers, cut out squares of crazy coloured paper to make place mats, use a piece of beautiful fabric as a runner up the middle of the table – the list is endless. Set your artistic side free!

When all the cooking is under control, set the table sooner rather than later, because it's not something you want to do at the last minute. From then on, it's down to the handy Work Plan alongside each menu to help you arrive smoothly at a delicious meal on the table.

I really want you to enjoy your kitchen and your cooking. It's great to go out, but some of the most memorable and enjoyable times will be in the comfort of your own home in relaxed company. If you have bought this book, you obviously have an interest in cooking, either as a beginner or an experienced cook with flair and creativity. So just turn the pages, choose the occasion and create your menu from the suggestions given. Shop and cook – yes, it's as simple as that. Oh, and don't forget to pour a drink, put on some music and enjoy your cooking.

tips and hints

Cooking is one of life's pleasures and it can really bring joy to a home. Cooking a good meal binds the love and friendship between family and friends, and helps create warm and kind memories. Entertaining needn't be daunting.

EASY ENTERTAINING

MAKE IT EASY ON YOURSELF

• If cooking is not your strong point, don't despair. Choose easy recipes and menus that won't challenge your skills – slowly your courage will grow and everyone will be amazed at your new-found talents. Don't be put off and remember that practice makes perfect.

PLANNING MENUS

• You will find menus that have been planned for you, with suggestions for a choice of wines. They will help with the first stumbling block of deciding what to serve. Sometimes there are a few choices, but most menus comprise balanced ideas without repetitive flavours, and tastes and textures to complement each other.

KITCHEN EQUIPMENT

• As soon as you have chosen the menu, check that you have all the necessary kitchen equipment. If not – buy, borrow or improvise.

SHOPPING LISTS

• It sounds obvious, but make a list. I find it easiest to separate the items into fish/meat, vegetables/fruit, groceries and drinks. Shop for dry goods in advance and buy the perishables on the day.

PLAN YOUR WORK

• Look at the Work Plan for each menu and make anything that can be cooked in advance. Chill the drinks the night before and open red wine an hour or two before serving: this lets it breathe so the flavours will improve and develop.

SET THE SCENE

• Set the table as far in advance as possible and set up any special little table details, such as place cards, vases, napkins, candles or fairy lights.

BUY THE BEST

- Buy the best you can afford. Think 'Quality not Quantity'.

- Buy the freshest, best-looking food – you will taste the difference.

THE BEST FLAVOURS

- Invest in a good pepper mill – freshly ground black pepper is by far the best.

- I prefer sea salt – Maldon is my favourite and no grinding is needed.

- A useful tip for juicing limes and even lemons is to microwave them on HIGH for 40 seconds, or warm in hot water – either method makes juicing a lot easier.

- Serve salads at room temperature to let the flavours come through.

- Chop herbs just before using so the flavours will be pungent and fresh.

- Plant a bay tree in your garden or in a pot – they are very hardy and nothing beats the flavour of a freshly picked bay leaf.

- Check your store cupboard – be ruthless and discard anything past its use-by date. Spices lose their flavour over time, so buy little and often. Dried beans, peas and lentils – believe it or not – also lose their quality if kept too long. So use or lose!

BAKING CAKES AND PASTRY

- Weigh and measure all the ingredients before you start. In baking, accuracy in measurement, oven heat and timing is the key to success. Always follow the recipe exactly.

- Leave plenty of time to preheat the oven before baking – at least 30 minutes is a good guide. (You can buy special oven thermometers to check that your oven temperature is accurate.)

- Don't try to make pastry in the middle of a hot day – at least do it in the early morning or late evening. The cooler your kitchen and your hands, the better the pastry will be.

- Always chill the butter when making pastry. Chill the dough for about 30 minutes before rolling, then chill the uncooked pastry case before baking. The dough heats up as you work on it – chilling lets it cool and rest so it won't shrink so much in the oven.

OILS

- Olive oil is not only the King of Oils, it is also a good all-round oil for all methods of cooking except Asian or Indian.

- For Indian and Asian cooking, I use sunflower oil, peanut oil or other good-quality non-olive oil.

- Avoid using oils labelled simply 'vegetable oil' – they are often extracted by heat treatment, a method that destroys many of the good things in oil.

- Always have a spout on the top of your bottle of oil – it limits the amount that pours out and gives you accurate direction when drizzling over dishes before serving.

KNIVES

- Have at least two good knives and sharpen them frequently.

- I use a whetstone rather than a steel to get a good sharp edge.

DRINKS

- Better to buy too much than too little – you can always use the extra at your next party.

- BUBBLY Allow ½–¾ bottle each (6 glasses in a bottle, or 8 if making cocktails).

- WINE Allow 1 bottle per person. In summer, allow 3 bottles of white to 1 of red.

- SPIRITS, COCKTAILS AND SPIRIT-BASED PUNCHES There are 16 measures in a 750 ml bottle of spirits. Allow 3 per person during a 2-hour party.

- MINERAL WATER AND SOFT DRINKS Don't forget the non-drinkers, 'designated drivers' and kids. Have lots and keep it cold!

everyday entertaining

Friends often quote complicated menus and ask me if cookbook authors are connected to the real world. Well, I am, and I want to help you to cook good food at home – food you will enjoy creating and everyone will love eating. For everyday entertaining, it is more important than ever to keep the menu simple and to be as prepared as possible.

The recipes in this section are designed to fit in with busy lives, and perfect for informal, quick or impromptu entertaining. Turn, for example, to Effortless Entertaining (page 40), Dinner in Advance (page 60) or Market Picnic (page 14), which I have devised to help minimize your time in the kitchen, while still giving stunning and delicious results.

My advice to you is to keep a well-stocked store cupboard. You don't want to be shopping for all the ingredients on a busy weekday, so if you have a few useful back-up supplies on hand, it only leaves the fresh ingredients to find on the day. Then just pick a menu, adapt and adjust it to suit your tastes or mood, pour yourself a drink and start cooking.

market picnic

market shopping

Treat yourself and take time out to visit your local market or farmers' market. Some even have the producers selling their own goods, so you can chat about the quality and taste. It's such a treat, as well as being a very sensual experience, to shop for food in a market. It often looks so raw and real, with the stallholders full of stories and love for their produce. Don't be afraid to ask questions – in my experience, they have a wealth of information that they are only too happy to share with their customers.

This menu is just to give you an idea of what you can buy to create an instant no-cook picnic. Delicacies will vary from place to place, but it's always fun to be adventurous and try something that you're not familiar with, be it a cheese, pâté, tart or simply an unusual bread.

MENU
SUGGESTIONS

Parma Ham

Salami

Potato and Tarragon Cake

Mixed Washed Leaves

Pâté en Croûte

Sliced Ham and Parsley Mousse

Pissaladière

Bread

Goats' Cheese

Peaches

Chocolate Opera Cake

Apple Custard Tart

Hazelnut Biscuits

Vanilla Yoghurts

TO DRINK

Apple Cider

THE WORK PLAN

on the day

- When you go to a market, always take plenty of small change. (I think it's rude to hand over a large note for a small bag of produce.)
- Have a large box or basket in which to carry your fresh treasures or, better still, take a strong friend to help gather and carry.
- What could be simpler: shop, travel to your chosen destination, spread out the rug, pour a drink and let everyone unwrap your treasures and enjoy your no-cook, inspirational, open air picnic.

the scene

After gathering your market purchases together in baskets, boxes and bags, find a quiet, shady spot under a tree, spread out a cloth and set out all the delicious produce for everyone to unwrap.

the style

This is really made by the surroundings and the goods you buy. Some producers take such pride in their packaging and presentation – beautiful sheets of waxed paper to wrap meats and cheeses, pretty boxes to protect tarts and cakes, crisp paper bags for bread and pretty baskets for fruit. All you need is a beautiful picnic blanket or cloth on which to set out your feast, plus cutlery and glasses.

mediterranean lunch

THE MENU

FOR 8 PEOPLE

Barbecued Tiger Prawns with Citrus Wedges

Summer Vegetable Salad

Haricot Bean and Tomato Salad

Baby Leaf Salad

Spring Garlic Dressing

Crusty Bread

Strawberry Tart

TO DRINK

Rosé

the scene

Just think of eating outside in the sunshine and cooking fresh prawns on a barbecue. Add some char-grilled vegetables bathed in extra virgin olive oil and a mixed summer leaf salad with fresh garlic dressing, then mop up all the juices with bread from a local bakery. All you need is a sunny day and this menu can be created in your own garden. The meal is very informal and perfect to serve at large, friendly gatherings. Your guests can help you create this feast. Put plates, napkins, knives and forks onto a tray and ask friends to set the table. Someone can help with the barbecue and others can make the salads.

the style

Decorate the table with simple flowers from the garden, wild grasses gathered from a meadow or bowls of ripe summer fruit, piled high. Provide a few little bowls with water and sliced lemons to dip and wash fingers, plus lots of napkins for laps and chins. Have everything you need set out on the table, so you don't have to keep getting up (and missing out on the laughter), then just graze your way through the afternoon.

summer vegetable salad

6 baby artichokes, stems removed

1 kg asparagus, ends trimmed

2 large red peppers, quartered and deseeded

5 courgettes, sliced lengthways

125 ml olive oil

freshly squeezed juice of 1 lemon

sea salt and freshly ground black pepper

serves 8

Bring a large saucepan of water to the boil. Add the artichokes and simmer for 30–40 minutes, or until tender.

Meanwhile, put the asparagus into a plastic bag with 3 tablespoons of the olive oil. Shake well. Heat a stove-top grill pan until hot, add the asparagus and cook for 5 minutes, turning frequently, until lightly charred. Remove and set aside.

Add the pepper pieces to the pan, skin side down, and cook for about 7 minutes, or until the skin is charred and blistered. Transfer to a small bowl, cover with a lid and let cool.

Add the courgettes and cook for 4 minutes on each side, until lightly charred.

Drain the artichokes and halve them lengthways. If they are small enough, they should have no 'choke', but scrape out the area with a teaspoon to make sure. Remove and discard the skins from the peppers and cut the flesh into strips.

Arrange all the vegetables in a large bowl, sprinkle with salt, pepper, olive oil and lemon juice, then serve.

barbecued tiger prawns with citrus wedges

For extra flavour and aroma, always grill prawns with their shells on. Toss them in olive oil before adding to the barbecue and cook just until the flesh is just opaque – don't overcook or they will be dry and tasteless. Buy as many prawns as you can afford – there will never be any left over.

2 kg tiger prawns, shell on

about 6 tablespoons olive oil

4 lemons or 6 limes, cut into wedges, to serve

serves 8

Put the prawns into a large bowl or plastic bag, pour over the olive oil and shake to coat. Cook on a preheated barbecue until the shells are red and the flesh is opaque, then serve on a large platter with lemon or lime wedges for squeezing.

haricot bean and tomato salad

750 g new potatoes, unpeeled

2 cans haricot or cannellini beans, about 410 g each, drained and rinsed

500 g ripe tomatoes, quartered

4 spring onions, sliced

a bunch of flat leaf parsley, chopped

4 tablespoons extra virgin olive oil

freshly squeezed juice of 1 lemon

sea salt and freshly ground black pepper

serves 8

Cook the potatoes in a large saucepan of boiling, salted water for about 20 minutes, or until tender when pierced with a knife. Drain. When cool enough to handle, cut into wedges and put into a large bowl.

Add the beans, tomatoes, onions and parsley. Sprinkle with olive oil, lemon juice, salt and pepper. Toss gently and serve.

baby leaf salad

Baby leaves (mesclun) with their contrasting flavours – sweet, crisp, bitter – are widely available in markets and supermarkets. When you wash salad leaves, always dry them in a salad spinner, as there's nothing worse than a soggy salad.

500 g small mixed salad leaves, washed and dried

spring garlic dressing (right)

serves 8

Check that all the leaves are clean. Trim off any dead ends and discard any droopy leaves. Put the leaves into a large bowl and serve the dressing separately.

spring garlic dressing

If you are lucky enough to find spring garlic use it to make this surprisingly mild salad dressing. Spring garlic bulbs are larger than usual and the most beautiful pink. This dressing doesn't need any mixing or shaking – serve it with a little spoon so guests can help themselves. It tastes great and looks like a work of art.

1 large garlic bulb, spring garlic if possible, finely sliced

7 tablespoons olive oil

2 tablespoons balsamic vinegar

sea salt and freshly ground black pepper

serves 8

Put the garlic into a small serving bowl. Add the oil and balsamic vinegar, with salt and pepper to taste, then serve.

THE WORK PLAN

the day before

- Make the strawberry tart case. Store in an airtight container.

on the day

- Cook the artichokes. Drain and let cool. Cook the remaining vegetables for the summer vegetable salad in the grill pan and assemble.
- Assemble the strawberry tart.
- Light the barbecue.
- Cook the potatoes.
- Make the bean and tomato salad.

just before serving

- Make the spring garlic dressing.
- Cook the prawns on the preheated barbecue.

strawberry tart

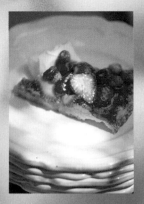

When any fruit is abundant and in season, I feel it just has to be used in a tart with sweet and crumbling pastry. This mixture of wild and farmed strawberries is just delicious – the tiny wild strawberries look so beautiful and are packed with flavour. If you can't find them, use the same weight in farmed. Any other soft fruit can be used, just make sure you pile the tart high with fruit.

Put the flour into a mixing bowl and add the butter. Using your fingertips, rub the butter into the flour until it looks like breadcrumbs. Add the sugar and mix. Make a well in the middle and add 2 of the egg yolks. Mix with a round-bladed knife, using cutting motions, until the mixture forms a ball, adding an extra egg yolk if needed. Dust your hands lightly with flour, bring the mixture together and transfer to a lightly floured, cool surface.

Roll out the pastry to just bigger than the tin. Line the tin with the pastry, prick all over with a fork and chill for 20 minutes. Cook in a preheated oven at 180°C (350°F) Gas 4 for 20 minutes, then reduce to 150°C (300°F) Gas 2 and cook for a further 20 minutes. Remove from the oven and let cool, then transfer to a flat serving plate and cover with clingfilm until needed.

Put the redcurrant jelly into a small saucepan and heat gently until thin and smooth. Remove and set aside to cool a little while you pile the strawberries into the cooked pastry case, cutting any very large berries into smaller pieces. Spoon the redcurrant jelly over the strawberries and serve with cream or Greek yoghurt mixed with honey.

300 g plain flour

200 g butter, cut into small pieces

150 g light brown sugar

2–3 egg yolks, beaten

200 g redcurrant jelly

250 g wild strawberries

750 g farmed strawberries, hulls removed

double cream or Greek yoghurt mixed with honey, to serve

a non-stick flan tin, 30 cm diameter

serves 8

autumn dinner

THE MENU

FOR 6 PEOPLE

Tuscan Bean and Spicy
Sausage Soup

Focaccia

Roasted Pheasant
Breasts with Bacon,
Shallots and
Mushrooms

Marbled Chocolate
Risotto

or

Fruit Crumbles

TO DRINK

Merlot, Italian-style red
such as Sangiovese

the scene

When the days start to draw in and the leaves fall from the trees, I must admit I get a little sad, so I cheer myself up by indulging in the fabulous seasonal foods available at this time of year. It's a great way to banish the cold weather blues.

the style

Move the table to the cosiest part of your home and create a snug feeling for enjoying the seasonal bounty. If you are lucky enough to have a fireplace, pull up a table and comfy armchairs in front of a roaring fire.

tuscan bean and spicy sausage soup

If you want to use dried, rather than canned, cannellini beans, soak them overnight, drain and put into a saucepan with water to cover. Bring to the boil and simmer for 10 minutes, then drain. Return to the pan, again with cold water to cover. Bring to the boil and simmer for 1 hour, removing any foam that rises to the surface. Stir occasionally.

2 tablespoons olive oil

2 red onions, chopped

2 garlic cloves, chopped

100 g pancetta, chopped

1 carrot, finely chopped

2 celery stalks, chopped

1 can cannellini beans, about 410 g, drained, or 200 g dried, cooked

3 spicy Italian sausages

1 litre chicken stock

1 bay leaf

a bunch of flat leaf parsley, chopped

sea salt and freshly ground black pepper

serves 6

Put the oil into a saucepan, heat well, then add the onion, garlic, pancetta, carrot and celery and cook over low heat for 10 minutes until softened but not browned. Add the beans, sausages, stock, bay leaf, salt and pepper. Bring to the boil, cover with a lid and simmer for 30 minutes. Skim off any excess fat, then remove the sausages and slice them diagonally. Return the sausages to the soup and add the parsley. Serve in large, heated soup plates.

focaccia

450 g strong plain flour

1 sachet (7 g) easy-blend dried yeast

125 ml virgin olive oil, plus extra for greasing and brushing

12 cherry tomatoes

leaves from a sprig of rosemary

coarse sea salt

a baking sheet, lightly greased with olive oil

serves 6

Put the flour and yeast into a food processor. With the motor on low speed, gradually add the oil and 300 ml warm water until the mixture forms a soft dough. Remove to a lightly floured surface and knead for 5 minutes. Transfer to the prepared baking sheet and, using your hands, spread it evenly to the edges. Brush all over with oil, push the cherry tomatoes and rosemary leaves lightly into the surface of the dough at regular intervals and sprinkle sea salt over the top. Cover with a damp, clean tea towel and put in a warm place for 40 minutes until doubled in size.

Bake in a preheated oven at 200°C (400°F) Gas 6 for 20 minutes, until golden.

THE WORK PLAN

the day before

- Make and cook the fruit crumbles.
- Make the soup, but don't slice the sausages or add the parsley.

on the day

- Make the focaccia.
- Wrap the pheasant breasts with bacon, prepare the shallots and mushrooms, cover and chill until 1 hour before cooking.
- Prepare the risotto ingredients, but don't cook until just before serving.

just before serving

- Reheat the soup, adding the sliced sausages and parsley.
- Cook the pheasant.
- Cook the risotto.
- Put the fruit crumbles into a preheated oven at 150°C (300°F) Gas 2 for 20 minutes.

roasted pheasant breasts with bacon, shallots and mushrooms

Depending on size, you may need two breasts per person – this is something you can decide when shopping, The look-and-choose, visual method is always best. If you are offered a choice between hen and cock pheasant, buy the hen – they have better breast meat and are plumper. Cooking a whole pheasant is more economical and will serve 2–3 people, but involves all that last-minute carving and it never looks as good.

6 plump pheasant breasts

12 slices smoked, rindless bacon

6 sprigs of thyme

3 fresh bay leaves, halved

25 g butter

1 tablespoon olive oil

12 shallots

100 ml dry sherry

6 portobello mushrooms, quartered

6 thick slices French bread

200 g watercress

sea salt and freshly cracked black pepper

serves 6

Remove the skin from the pheasant breasts and discard it. Wrap 2 slices of bacon around each breast, inserting a sprig of thyme and half a bay leaf between the pheasant and the bacon.

Put the butter and oil into a large roasting tin and set on top of the stove over high heat. Add the pheasant breasts, shallots, sherry, mushrooms, salt and pepper. Turn the pheasant breasts in the mixture until they are well coated. Cook at the top of a preheated oven at 190°C (375°F) Gas 5 for 25 minutes. Remove from the oven and let rest for 5 minutes. Put the bread onto plates, then add the watercress, mushrooms, shallots and pheasant. Spoon over any cooking juices and serve.

Trust me: this chocolate risotto is the best. Soft grains of rice gently cooked in milk, swathed in melted chocolate — don't say you aren't tempted!

marbled chocolate risotto

This dish is so wicked — it's my 21st century version of rice pudding. For a real treat, soak the sultanas in brandy or whisky for 2 hours first.

600 ml milk

25 g unrefined caster sugar

50 g butter

125 g risotto rice, such as arborio or carnaroli

50 g hazelnuts, chopped

50 g sultanas

50 g milk chocolate, grated

50 g dark chocolate (70 per cent cocoa solids), grated

serves 6

Put the milk and sugar into a saucepan and heat until just simmering. Melt the butter in a large, heavy-based saucepan, add the rice and stir well to coat the grains. Add a ladle of the warm milk and mix well. When the milk has been absorbed, add more and continue, stirring frequently, until it has all been added and the rice is soft. This will take about 12–15 minutes. Add the hazelnuts and sultanas and mix well. Remove from the heat and add the grated chocolate, stirring briefly to create a marbled effect. Serve at once.

fruit crumbles

My favourite crumbles are always made with red berries, because they are so juicy and delicious. However, I always include a cooking apple to add a little texture.

150 g plain flour

75 g butter, cut into small pieces

100 g soft brown sugar

50 g rolled oats

500 g mixed berries and fruit, such as blackberries, redcurrants, blackcurrants, raspberries, strawberries, plums or blush gooseberries, pitted if necessary

1 large cooking apple, such as Bramley, cored, peeled and sliced

50 g unrefined caster sugar

cream or real custard (page 53), to serve

6 ramekins

serves 6

To make the crumble topping, put the flour into a bowl and rub in the butter with your fingertips until it disappears into the flour. Add the brown sugar and oats and mix well.

Remove and discard any stalks from the berries and fruits. Cut into even pieces, if necessary, and put into a bowl. Stir in the apple. Divide the fruit between the ramekins, then sprinkle with caster sugar and the crumble topping. Cook in a preheated oven at 180°C (350°F) Gas 4 for about 40 minutes until golden and bubbling. Serve with cream or real custard.

the scene

For a midweek after-work supper, this menu is very flexible, with an easy salad, the risotto, then the option of baked apples or toasted oat yoghurts, according to taste and what's in the cupboard. It's all quick to prepare, to fit in with a busy working day.

the style

Sit around a simply clad table, put the food in the middle and tuck in. Serve the risotto straight from the pan.

express dining

THE MENU

SERVES 4

Poached Egg and Anchovy Salad

Classic Risotto

Toasted Oat Yoghurt and Crushed Red Berries

or

Baked Stuffed Apples with Butterscotch

TO DRINK

Pinot Grigio, crisp Riesling, Sangiovese, Merlot

poached egg and anchovy salad

Using a hand-held stick blender is a quick and easy way to get a good, emulsified dressing. I always make double the amount because this dressing is so good.

Put the mixed leaves into a large bowl and add the capers. Put the anchovies into a small bowl and add the mustard powder, vinegar and oil. Blend, with a hand-held stick blender, until emulsified.

Fill a large, shallow saucepan with hot water, heat to a gentle simmer and crack each egg into a separate cup. Stir the water in one direction to create a whirlpool. Gently slip each egg into the water and return to a gentle simmer. Cover, remove the pan from the heat and let stand for 6 minutes for softly poached eggs.

Meanwhile, reserve a few of the chives and add the remainder to the salad. Sprinkle with salt and pepper. Reserve a little of the dressing for serving and pour the remainder over the salad. Toss well and put onto serving plates. Remove the eggs from the water using a slotted spoon and dry underneath the spoon with kitchen paper. Put an egg on top of each salad. Spoon over a little dressing, top with a few chives and serve.

200 g mixed salad leaves, washed and dried

1 tablespoon capers, drained and rinsed

4 anchovy fillets in oil, drained and finely chopped

1 teaspoon English mustard powder

1 tablespoon white wine vinegar

3 tablespoons extra virgin olive oil

4 eggs

sea salt and freshly ground black pepper

a bunch of chives, chopped, to serve

serves 4

THE WORK PLAN

the day before

- Make the butterscotch sauce, cover and chill. (Reheat in a saucepan.)

on the day

- Prepare and stuff the apples, cover and set aside.
- Make the toasted oat yoghurts, cover and chill.

just before serving

- Make the salad dressing, cook the eggs and assemble the salad.
- Bake the apples.
- Prepare and cook the risotto.

classic risotto

If you are a keen cook you may make all your own stock, which is brilliant and I admire you, but I only do it sometimes! Luckily, it's possible to buy good stock.

1 litre chicken or vegetable stock

75 g butter

1 tablespoon olive oil

4 shallots, finely chopped

400 g risotto rice, such as arborio or carnaroli

1/2 teaspoon saffron threads

150 ml dry vermouth

125 g freshly grated Parmesan cheese, plus extra to serve

sea salt and freshly ground black pepper

serves 4

Put the stock into a saucepan and heat until simmering. Put 50 g of the butter into a large saucepan, add the oil and heat until the butter has melted. Add the shallots and sauté for 5 minutes, until softened but not browned.

Add the rice and stir until coated. Add the saffron and just enough hot stock to cover the rice. Simmer gently, stirring frequently and adding more stock as it is absorbed by the rice.

When all the stock has been added and almost absorbed, about 12–15 minutes, add the vermouth, Parmesan and remaining butter. Add salt and pepper to taste and simmer until the rice is soft and the sauce rich and creamy. Sprinkle with Parmesan and serve.

toasted oat yoghurt and crushed red berries

Baking the oats adds a caramel crunch to this simple pudding. If you don't have the berries, use whatever fruit you have already – bananas, apples, pears, peaches or nectarines are all good.

50 g rolled oats

20 g fine brown sugar

300 g mixed berries

200 ml Greek yoghurt

4 tablespoons runny honey

a baking sheet, lined with bakewell paper

serves 4

Put the rolled oats and sugar into a bowl and mix. Sprinkle evenly over the baking sheet and put under a preheated grill. Toast until golden and caramelized, then remove and let cool on the sheet.

Put half the berries into a bowl and coarsely crush with the back of a spoon. Add the yoghurt and toasted oats and mix lightly until marbled. Spoon into glasses and top with the remaining berries and honey. Chill until ready to serve.

I can never choose between the toasted oat yoghurts and baked stuffed apples – they are both so perfect and simple. If you are like me, make both.

50 g butter

3 tablespoons brown sugar

50 g raisins

100 g dried cranberries

100 g dried cherries

6 cooking apples, such as Bramleys, cored

1 cinnamon stick, broken lengthways into 6 thin strips

BUTTERSCOTCH

50 g butter

125 g light brown sugar

150 g golden syrup

125 ml double cream

an ovenproof dish, big enough to fit the apples, lightly buttered

serves 4

baked stuffed apples with butterscotch

Butterscotch is absolutely wicked stuff, but occasionally a wicked must. It can be made 2 weeks in advance and stored in a screwtop jar in the refrigerator. Try it hot or cold with ice cream, bananas or chocolate sponge – it's always a winner for people with a sweet tooth. I always make 2 extra apples, for seconds.

Put the butter and sugar into a bowl, beat until creamy, then stir in the dried fruits. Using a small, sharp knife, score the skin all the way around the middle of each apple, to prevent them bursting. Put the apples into the prepared dish, stuff with the dried fruit mixture and put a piece of cinnamon into each. Bake on the middle shelf of a preheated oven at 190°C (375°F) Gas 5 for 20 minutes, then reduce to 150°C (300°F) Gas 2 and bake for a further 25 minutes, until soft and bubbling.

To make the butterscotch, put the butter, sugar and syrup into a saucepan. Heat slowly over low heat until melted, then gently simmer for 5 minutes. Remove from the heat and gradually add the cream, stirring constantly, until it has all been added and the sauce is smooth. Serve spooned over the baked apples.

the scene

Move tables and chairs out into the garden
– standing and having to balance plates and
glasses can spoil a delicious meal. Otherwise,
you can put large tablecloths or blankets on
the ground and provide big soft cushions.

the style

When the sun comes out and the garden is
full of flowers, those barbecues emerge from
everybody's garden sheds. Barbecues come
in all shapes and sizes and, although the gas
ones are convenient and easy, I do think that,
for real barbecue flavour, you need coals or
wood. The menu is mixed mezze-style, with
food to suit all tastes.

THE WORK PLAN

the day before

- Make the pastry cases for the tarts and
  store in a cool place.
- Marinate the lamb overnight.
- Slow-roast the tomatoes for the salsa,
  cover and chill.

on the day

- Assemble and cook the fruit tarts.
- Make the bean salad, cover and store at
  room temperature.
- Cook the croutons and lardons for the
  frisée salad.
- Preheat the barbecue. This will take at
  least an hour.

just before serving

- Barbecue the lamb and put the chicken
  wings into the oven to roast.
- Make the salsa for the swordfish and
  prepare the aubergines for the barbecue.
- Barbecue the aubergines and courgettes.
- Make the couscous salad.
- Assemble the aubergine and feta salad
  and the frisée salad.
- Barbecue the swordfish.
- Add the sticky sauce to the chicken.

relaxed garden barbecue

swordfish with salsa

Swordfish is brought to life with this delicious half-cooked salsa. Slow-roasting softens the tomatoes and intensifies their flavour. This salsa is a much-loved recipe that I serve with many different fish and meat dishes. It's also great served on a bowl of fresh pasta such as ravioli.

500 g cherry tomatoes

2 red onions, finely chopped

1/2 teaspoon crushed dried chillies

a large bunch of flat leaf parsley, chopped

6 tablespoons olive oil

freshly squeezed juice of 2 limes

8 swordfish steaks, 100 g each

sea salt and freshly ground pepper

serves 8

To make the salsa, put the tomatoes into a roasting tin and cook in a preheated oven at 150°C (300°F) Gas 2 for 1 hour. Remove and let cool.

Transfer to a bowl, add the onions, dried chillies, parsley, oil, lime juice, salt and pepper. Mix well.

Sprinkle the swordfish steaks with salt and pepper. Cook over medium heat on a preheated barbecue for 4–6 minutes on each side, depending on thickness, until just cooked through. Serve with the salsa.

honeyed chicken wings

These really should be called Last Lick Chicken Wings – anyone who eats them removes every morsel of flavour and sticky meat. Just watch out that they don't burn in the oven.

16 chicken wings

200 ml runny honey

100 ml sweet chilli sauce

sea salt and freshly ground black pepper

a bunch of radishes, trimmed, to serve (optional)

serves 8

Put the chicken wings into an oiled roasting tin and cook in a preheated oven at 200°C (400°F) Gas 6 for 40 minutes, turning them after 20 minutes so they brown evenly all over.

Meanwhile, put the honey and sweet chilli sauce into a small saucepan. Add salt and pepper to taste and bring to the boil. Pour the sauce over the chicken, mix well and let cool. Serve with radishes, if using.

barbecued courgettes

8 courgettes, cut lengthways into 1 cm slices

olive oil

balsamic vinegar

salt and freshly ground black pepper

serves 8

Cook the courgette slices over medium heat on a preheated barbecue for 3–4 minutes on each side, until lightly charred. Remove to a plate and sprinkle with oil, vinegar, salt and pepper. Serve hot, warm or cold.

turmeric lamb fillet with couscous salad

There are two cuts of lamb fillet which can be used for this dish; one is from the eye of the cutlets and is truly melt-in-the-mouth, but expensive. The other is from the neck: it's more marbled with fat and far cheaper. I don't think I have to tell you, but my favourite is the expensive, every time!

TURMERIC LAMB

3 teaspoons ground turmeric

1 teaspoon ground cinnamon

3 teaspoons medium curry powder

2 garlic cloves, chopped

3 tablespoons olive oil

4 tablespoons runny honey

1.5 kg lamb fillets

sea salt and freshly ground black pepper

COUSCOUS SALAD

375 g couscous

1/2 teaspoon saffron threads

25 g butter

2 tablespoons olive oil

4 onions, sliced

1 garlic clove, chopped

100 g shelled pistachio nuts, coarsely chopped

grated zest and freshly squeezed juice of 2 unwaxed lemons

a large bunch of coriander, chopped

sea salt and freshly ground black pepper

serves 8

Put the turmeric, cinnamon, curry powder, garlic, oil and honey into a bowl, add salt and pepper to taste and stir well. Trim any excess fat off the lamb fillets and rub the spice mixture all over. Transfer to a dish, cover and chill overnight.

To make the couscous salad, put the couscous and saffron into a large bowl. Pour over 400 ml boiling water, mix and set aside for 15 minutes until all the liquid has been absorbed.

Meanwhile, heat the butter and oil in a large frying pan, add the onions and cook for 8 minutes until golden and slightly frizzled. Add the garlic and cook for a further 2 minutes, then add the onions and garlic to the prepared couscous.

Add the pistachio nuts, lemon zest and juice, coriander and salt and pepper to taste, mix well and set aside.

Cook the lamb fillets on a hot preheated barbecue for about 25 minutes for medium rare, turning them frequently and basting with any extra marinade. Remove to a board, slice and serve with the couscous salad.

classic frisée and bacon salad

2 frisée lettuces, leaves separated

2 shallots, finely chopped

2 tablespoons olive oil, plus extra to serve

500 g dry-cured bacon, chopped

2 tablespoons red wine vinegar

a bunch of basil, leaves torn

sea salt and freshly ground black pepper

serves 8

Put the lettuce into a large serving bowl and add the shallots.

Heat the olive oil in a large frying pan, add the bacon and cook until brown and crispy. If serving immediately, add to the lettuce and shallots. Otherwise, remove to a plate and let cool.

Just before serving, add the bacon, olive oil, vinegar, basil, salt and pepper to the bowl. Toss well and serve.

white and green bean salad

The ingredients for this salad are very flexible: haricot beans or chickpeas could be used in place of the butter beans, and other green beans – such as mangetout, sugar snaps or sliced runner beans – in place of the fine green beans.

3 tablespoons olive oil

1 tablespoon balsamic vinegar

2 cans butter beans, 410 g each, drained and rinsed

300 g fine green beans, trimmed

100 g pumpkin seeds

sea salt and freshly ground black pepper

serves 8

Put the oil and vinegar into a large serving bowl. Stir in the butter beans and set aside. Cook the green beans in a saucepan of boiling, salted water for 3 minutes. Drain, refresh in several changes of cold water until cool, then drain again. Add the green beans and pumpkin seeds to the bowl and stir. Sprinkle with salt and pepper and serve.

baked seasonal fruit tarts with pouring cream

Once the rich, simple pastry has been made, these delicious tarts are very easy. You just fill with seasonal fruit and bake them slowly. Choose from apricots, plums, cherries, apples, blueberries, peaches and nectarines. Don't worry if the pastry breaks as you line the tins – just patch any holes or cracks with the trimmings. It will be topped with lovely fruit, so no one will know!

600 g plain flour, plus extra for dusting

600 g softened butter, cut into pieces

180 g icing sugar, plus extra for dusting

3 egg yolks

1.5 kg fruit, deseeded if necessary

500 ml single cream, to serve

2 loose-based flan tins, 28 cm diameter

serves 8

To make the pastry, put the flour, butter and icing sugar into a food processor and blend briefly. Add the egg yolks and blend until the mixture forms a ball. Divide in half, wrap both pieces in clingfilm and chill for 40 minutes.

Put one piece of pastry onto a cool, lightly floured surface and gently knead to a flat disc. Roll out into a circle large enough to fit the flan tin, dusting lightly with flour to stop the pastry sticking to the surface. Roll the pastry around a floured rolling pin and unroll over the flan tin. Gently press the pastry into the tin, pressing out any air pockets, then roll the pin over the top of the tin to remove any excess pastry. Repeat with the remaining pastry and flan tin, cover and chill for 25 minutes.

Prepare the fruit and slice, halve or leave whole, depending on size, and arrange in the chilled pastry cases. Working from the outside in, cram in all the fruit (it will shrink while cooking). Cook in a preheated oven at 180°C (350°F) Gas 4 for 35 minutes, then reduce to 150°C (300°F) Gas 2 and cook for a further 55 minutes until the pastry is golden and crisp. Remove and dust generously with icing sugar. Serve hot, warm or cold with pouring cream.

aubergine and feta salad

If you have a specialist Greek or Middle Eastern food shop near you, buy feta cheese there: they will have a good range of varying sharpness and texture. Taste and choose the one for you.

4 tablespoons olive oil

1 teaspoon ground cumin

1 teaspoon ground coriander

3 medium aubergines, cut into 2.5 cm slices

200 g feta cheese, crumbled

100 g pine nuts, toasted in a dry frying pan

a bunch of mint, chopped

sea salt and freshly ground black pepper

serves 8

Put the oil, cumin and coriander into a bowl, add salt and pepper to taste and mix. Brush both sides of the aubergine slices with the spiced oil and cook on a hot preheated barbecue for 3–4 minutes on each side, until soft and lightly charred. Transfer to a large bowl, then stir in the feta, pine nuts and mint. Serve warm, at room temperature or cold.

effortless entertaining

the scene

Visual appeal is important to this cook, but the cooking has to be effortless too. The menu is simple and easy to prepare, and looks oh-so-perfect in this stylish setting.

the style

Beautiful and slightly serene, this is for the cook who would rather concentrate, not on elaborate cooking, but on the table – all the latest looks for china and cutlery. The food sits beautifully in this amazing setting – one for the style guru!

THE WORK PLAN

the day before

- Make and cook the apple bake or roast the peaches and stew the rhubarb.
- Prepare the cream, cover and chill.

on the day

- Roast the aubergines and tomatoes and make the dressing.
- Peel and chop the tomatoes to go with the guinea fowl.

just before serving

- Trim and cook the artichokes.
- Assemble the salad and grill the Parma ham.
- Cook the spaghetti and guinea fowl.
- Assemble the peaches and rhubarb.

THE MENU

FOR 4 PEOPLE

Easy Artichokes

Roasted Aubergine and Parma Ham Salad

Guinea Fowl and Asparagus Spaghetti

Norwegian Apple Bake

or

Roasted Peaches with Rhubarb and Mascarpone Cream

TO DRINK

Chardonnay, Zinfandel

easy artichokes

Put out extra napkins – eating artichokes is a hands-on experience!

4 medium artichokes, stems removed

extra virgin olive oil, to serve

serves 4

Put the artichokes into a large saucepan, stem side down, cover with water and bring to the boil. Simmer for 40 minutes, until an outer leaf pulls away easily. Drain well and turn the artichokes upside down in a colander to cool and drain off excess water. Serve warm, with olive oil for dipping.

roasted aubergine and parma ham salad

Parma ham makes the best crispy bacon any kitchen can produce, so start cooking and impress with your relaxed and easy new-found kitchen skills.

200 g cherry tomatoes

2 small aubergines, sliced lengthways

2 tablespoons olive oil

4 slices Parma ham

a bunch of rocket

salt and freshly ground black pepper

DRESSING

1 tablespoon balsamic vinegar

1 tablespoon Dijon mustard

3 tablespoons extra virgin olive oil

salt and freshly ground black pepper

serves 4

Slice off and discard the top of each tomato, then put them, cut side up, into an oiled roasting tin. Add the aubergines. Sprinkle with the olive oil, salt and pepper. Cook in a preheated oven at 180°C (350°F) Gas 4 for 15 minutes, then reduce to 150°C (300°F) Gas 2 and cook for a further 15 minutes, until the tomatoes have burst their skins. Remove from the oven and set aside. Cook the Parma ham under a hot grill for about 3 minutes on each side, until crisp.

To make the dressing, put the vinegar and mustard into a small bowl and mix until smooth. Gradually add the oil, mixing well, then add salt and pepper to taste. Arrange the rocket and roasted aubergines and tomatoes on plates and spoon over the dressing. Top with the Parma ham and serve warm or at room temperature.

2 large tomatoes

300 g dried spaghetti

4 guinea fowl breasts, or
chicken breasts, 100 g each

300 g asparagus, trimmed

200 g fine green beans

4 tablespoons olive oil,
plus extra to serve

75 g black olives,
pitted and chopped

sea salt and freshly ground
black pepper

fresh shavings of
Parmesan cheese, to serve

serves 4

guinea fowl and asparagus spaghetti

This is my one-pot-wonder, and I just love the combination of clean and fresh flavours.
The spaghetti absorbs the rich stock, so tastes good and looks fantastic. Try this method
using other boneless cuts of meat or fish that need very quick cooking.

Cut a cross in the top of each tomato, put into a bowl and cover with boiling water. Drain after 30 seconds, then skin and chop.

Bring a large saucepan of water to the boil and add the spaghetti. Stir, then put the guinea fowl breasts on top of the spaghetti. Cover with a lid and simmer for 8 minutes, then add the asparagus and beans. Replace the lid and cook for a further 3 minutes, until the spaghetti and guinea fowl are cooked. Drain, reserving the cooking liquid for a soup or sauce.

Transfer the guinea fowl to a carving board and cover loosely with foil. Return the spaghetti to the saucepan over medium heat and add the oil, olives, tomatoes, salt and pepper. Cook, stirring constantly, for 2 minutes, then transfer to warmed serving plates. Slice the guinea fowl and arrange on top of the spaghetti. Top with Parmesan shavings, drizzle with olive oil, sprinkle with salt and pepper, then serve.

norwegian apple bake

This is such a good standby pudding – usually, you will have all the dry ingredients in your cupboard. You can use any kind of apples, pears or even plums.

2 eggs

250 g unrefined caster sugar

100 g butter

150 ml milk

4 cooking apples, cored, peeled and sliced

175 g self-raising flour

1/2 teaspoon freshly grated nutmeg

thick cream or vanilla ice cream, to serve

a shallow ovenproof dish, 30 cm diameter, buttered

serves 4

Put the eggs into a large bowl, add 200 g of the sugar and whisk until stiff and creamy. Put the butter and milk into a saucepan and heat gently until the butter has melted. Meanwhile, arrange the apple slices in the buttered dish.

Gradually add the hot milk and butter to the egg mixture, whisking well. Fold in the flour to make a smooth batter. Pour the mixture over the apples, then sprinkle with the remaining sugar and the nutmeg. Bake in a preheated oven at 180°C (350°F) Gas 5 for 20–25 minutes until puffed and golden. Serve hot or cold with scoops of thick cream or vanilla ice cream.

roasted peaches with rhubarb and mascarpone cream

Roasted peaches have been around a long time, but I have added an extra twist with the stewed rhubarb and cream.

4 soft, juicy peaches or nectarines, halved crossways and pitted

275 g rhubarb, chopped into 2 cm slices

4 tablespoons double cream

75 g unrefined caster sugar

4 tablespoons mascarpone cheese

a baking dish, lightly buttered

serves 4

Put the peach halves into the buttered baking dish, skin side down, and roast at the top of a preheated oven at 200°C (400°F) Gas 6 for 15 minutes until caramelized and softened.

Meanwhile, put the rhubarb into a small saucepan, add 1 tablespoon water and heat until bubbling. Reduce the heat to low, cover with a lid and cook for 10 minutes. Remove from the heat and set aside to cool, with the lid on.

Put the cream into a bowl and whip lightly. Add the sugar and mascarpone and mix until smooth. Add the stewed rhubarb and stir briefly, adding more sugar if needed. Serve with the roasted peaches, with any juices spooned over the top.

THE MENU

FOR 8 PEOPLE

Baked Fennel with
Shallots and Spicy
Dressing

Lamb Navarin

Garlic and Parsley
Bread

Warm Chocolate
and Coffee Pudding

TO DRINK

Syrah (Shiraz),
Merlot, Cabernet
Sauvignon

2 fennel bulbs

4 shallots, chopped

1 teaspoon unrefined
caster sugar

3 tablespoons olive oil

1 garlic clove, crushed
and chopped

2.5 cm fresh ginger,
peeled and chopped

a bunch of spring onions,
sliced

1 tablespoon sesame oil

freshly squeezed juice of
1 lemon

1/2 teaspoon chilli powder

sea salt and freshly
ground black pepper

serves 8

baked fennel with shallots and spicy dressing

Fennel is a beautiful vegetable, and very versatile. You can roast it with
other vegetables or serve raw in a salad, finely sliced or chopped. The
fennel bulbs come in two shapes – very slim and tall, or plump and round.
Guess what: the slim ones are male and the plump ones female!

Cut the base off the fennel bulbs and trim the tops. Cut each bulb lengthways into
4 and cut out the hard core. Put into an ovenproof dish and add the shallots, sugar
and 2 tablespoons of the olive oil. Mix well and bake in a preheated oven at 160°C
(325°F) Gas 3 for 30 minutes.

Put the remaining olive oil into a small saucepan, add the garlic and ginger and cook
over very low heat for 10 minutes. Add the spring onions, sesame oil, lemon juice,
chilli powder and salt and pepper to taste. Gently bring to a simmer, then pour over
the roasted fennel, mix well and serve with all the juices.

warming winter supper

the scene

Lazy suppers of rich and comforting food can
banish all thoughts of beaches and bikinis. So
indulge in this menu of warming, slow-cooked
dishes, just perfect for the long winter evenings.
I call it duvet food.

the style

This simple supper needs a table with a
comfortable and homely feel, so put out chunky
place mats, farmhouse china and traditional
cutlery. This is humble and wholesome eating
at its best.

lamb navarin

A fantastic dish that can be made in advance, then just finished off on the day: this makes your life easier and also improves the flavour of the dish. All the vegetables can be altered to suit your taste: try leeks, cauliflower and broccoli florets, asparagus, parsnips, turnips, pumpkin or sweet potatoes – the list is endless.

2 kg boneless leg or shoulder of lamb, cubed

3 tablespoons olive oil

3 tablespoons plain flour

1 litre vegetable stock

2 cans chopped tomatoes, 410 g each

1 tablespoon tomato purée

150 ml red wine

2 bay leaves

2 sprigs of marjoram

1/2 teaspoon smoked paprika

2 garlic cloves, crushed and chopped

8 shallots

300 g baby carrots, scrubbed

300 g new potatoes, scrubbed

3 celery stalks, cut into chunks

100 g flat beans, chopped

50 g curly kale or spring greens, coarsely chopped

sea salt and freshly ground black pepper

serves 8

THE WORK PLAN

the day before

- Prepare the lamb up to the point specified in the recipe. Cover and chill.
- Make the chocolate and coffee pudding and sauce, cover and chill.

on the day

- Make the spicy dressing.

just before serving

- Reheat the lamb, add the vegetables and finish cooking.
- Cook the fennel.
- Make the garlic bread.
- Reheat the pudding and sauce (in the microwave if you have one – the pudding for 6–7 minutes on MED, the sauce for 3 minutes on MED).

Trim any excess fat from the lamb. Heat the oil in a large flameproof casserole or saucepan, add the lamb and cook briefly until browned all over. Depending on the size of the pan, you may have to do this in batches.

Return all the meat to the pan, sprinkle with a fine dusting of flour, mix well and repeat until all the flour has been incorporated. Add the vegetable stock, tomatoes, tomato purée, wine, herbs, paprika, garlic and shallots. Mix well and bring to the boil. Reduce the heat and simmer gently for 1 hour, stirring from time to time. Add salt and pepper to taste.

(If making in advance, prepare up to this point, let cool, then chill overnight.) Add the carrots, potatoes and celery and cook for 15 minutes. Add the beans and curly kale or greens and stir gently. Cover with a lid and cook for a further 5 minutes, then serve with the garlic and parsley bread.

garlic and parsley bread

Everyone loves this easy bread, ideal for mopping up all those juices. It can be made with other breads, so choose your family favourite.

2 loaves ciabatta bread, split lengthways

3–4 garlic cloves, finely chopped

a bunch of flat leaf parsley, chopped

1/2 teaspoon crushed dried chillies

olive oil

sea salt and freshly ground black pepper

serves 8

Sprinkle the garlic, parsley, dried chillies, salt and pepper evenly over the opened bread halves. Drizzle generously with olive oil, then cook under a preheated grill until golden. Cut the bread into chunks and serve at once with the lamb navarin.

warm chocolate and coffee pudding

This pudding can be made in advance, then just reheated on the day. Don't scrimp on the chocolate sauce ingredients: they make a thick, rich and glossy sauce that will become one of your prized favourites. You can also serve it with poached pears, ice cream or other puddings.

1 teaspoon instant coffee

175 g butter

175 g unrefined caster sugar

2 large eggs

225 g self-raising flour

50 g cocoa powder

single cream, to serve

CHOCOLATE SAUCE

100 g plain chocolate (70 per cent cocoa solids), broken into pieces

100 g butter

50 g unrefined caster sugar

200 ml double cream

a pudding basin, 1 litre, buttered

foil, buttered, or greaseproof paper

serves 8

Put the coffee into a small cup, add 1 teaspoon of boiling water and stir to dissolve. Put 10 cm water into a saucepan large enough to hold the pudding basin. Put the butter and sugar into a bowl and, using an electric whisk, beat until creamy, light and very pale. Add the eggs and coffee and beat again.

Sift in the flour and cocoa powder and fold with a large metal spoon, adding a little milk if the mixture seems very stiff. Transfer to the prepared pudding basin and cover tightly with the buttered foil or greaseproof paper. Put into the saucepan of water, cover with a lid and bring to the boil. Reduce the heat and simmer for 1½ hours, checking the water level from time to time. Remove the bowl from the saucepan and carefully turn out the pudding onto a large plate. Serve hot or warm with the chocolate sauce and single cream.

To make the sauce, put the chocolate, butter, sugar and cream into a small saucepan. Heat gently, stirring frequently, until melted. Remove from the heat and set aside until ready to serve.

THE MENU

FOR 4 PEOPLE

**Rich Root Soup
with Green Tarragon
Drizzle**

**Poached Mushrooms
with Egg Noodles**

**Roasted Pumpkin,
Red Onions, Baby
Potatoes and Fennel
with Chickpeas
in Tomato Sauce**

Parmesan Biscuits

**Blackberry and
Apple Pie with
Real Custard**

TO DRINK

**Sauvignon Blanc,
Gamay**

country vegetarian lunch

the scene

Easy, relaxed, low-key entertaining with really good friends means the chatter and laughter are flowing. This menu is a celebration of garden or market produce, using beautiful, colourful vegetables just bursting with life and flavour. Get back to nature and enjoy the bounty of the countryside.

the style

Think farmers' market or kitchen garden, then keep the rustic look and extend it to your table. This isn't the time to worry about matching plates or neat presentation – use mixed china and chunky utensils and gather flowers and herbs from the garden to add to that country feeling.

THE WORK PLAN

the day before

- Make the soup and tomato sauce, cover and chill.
- Make the pastry, wrap and chill.
- Make the Parmesan biscuits, store in an airtight container.

on the day

- Assemble and cook the pie.
- Make the custard, cover with clingfilm.

just before serving

- Prepare and roast the vegetables.
- Make the poached mushrooms.
- Make the tarragon drizzle.
- Reheat the tomato sauce.
- Reheat the custard.

rich root soup with green tarragon drizzle

In the cold of the winter, a thick, rich soup is a delight every time – serve it with lots of warm, freshly baked bread and cold butter. The tarragon drizzle transforms this rather homely old-fashioned soup into something stylish and modern!

Put the oil into a large saucepan, heat gently, add the onion, garlic and celery and cook for 5 minutes. Add the parsnip, swede and carrot and cook for 3 minutes. Mix the bouillon powder with 1.5 litres boiling water and add to the vegetables. Add salt and pepper to taste, bring to the boil and simmer for 35 minutes, until the vegetables are tender. Remove from the heat and blend until smooth.

To make the drizzle, put the tarragon into a bowl and add the lemon juice and oil. Using a hard-held stick blender, blend until smooth. Ladle the hot soup into bowls, add a swirl of tarragon drizzle and serve.

1 tablespoon olive oil

2 onions, chopped

1 garlic clove, chopped

3 celery stalks, chopped

400 g parsnips, chopped

400 g swede, chopped

400 g carrots, chopped

3 1/2 teaspoons good quality vegetable bouillon powder

sea salt and freshly ground black pepper

GREEN TARRAGON DRIZZLE

a bunch of tarragon, finely chopped

freshly squeezed juice of 1/2 lemon

4 tablespoons olive oil

serves 4

poached mushrooms with egg noodles

The purity and natural flavours of this noodle dish
will make you feel very healthy! Try using tofu instead
of mushrooms, or a piece of haddock fillet with its
skin on, or even a chicken breast.

4 portobello mushrooms

4 baby leeks, trimmed

4 shallots

2 bay leaves

200 g dried egg noodles

2 courgettes, sliced into rounds

100 g baby sweetcorn, trimmed

100 g flat beans, sliced

100 g spinach, washed and chopped

1 tablespoon soy sauce

sea salt and freshly ground black pepper

Serves 4

Put the mushrooms into a large saucepan
and add the leeks, shallots, bay leaves, salt
and pepper. Add water to cover and heat
until simmering. Cover with a lid and cook
for 20 minutes. Add the noodles, adding
extra water to cover if necessary. Add the
courgettes, sweetcorn, beans, spinach
and soy sauce. Simmer for a further
4 minutes, until the noodles and all the
vegetables are cooked. Serve in bowls
with a ladle of the cooking juices.

parmesan biscuits

275 g Parmesan cheese, grated

*a baking sheet, lined with baking
parchment*

makes 20

Pile teaspoons of the grated Parmesan
onto the lined baking sheet and flatten
gently to give equal rounds. Bake in a
preheated oven at 190°C (375°F) Gas 5
for 5 minutes. Remove the paper from the
baking sheet with the biscuits still on it.
Replace with another sheet of paper and
repeat with the remaining cheese. Serve
with the roasted vegetables.

roasted pumpkin, red onions, baby potatoes and fennel with chickpeas in tomato sauce

An easy dish. The tomato sauce can be made the
night before – in fact it actually improves overnight.

1 butternut squash or
1/2 pumpkin, cut into
wedges, skin left on
and seeds left in

3 small red onions,
cut into wedges

8 baby new potatoes,
halved

2 fennel bulbs,
trimmed and cut into
wedges

3 tablespoons olive oil

1 can chickpeas,
410 g, drained and
rinsed

sea salt and freshly
ground black pepper

TOMATO SAUCE

2 tablespoons olive oil

1 onion, chopped

2 celery stalks,
chopped

1 leek, chopped

1 garlic clove, chopped

1 can chopped
tomatoes, 410 g

1 tablespoon tomato
purée

100 ml red wine

sea salt and freshly
ground black pepper

serves 4

Put the pumpkin or squash, onion, potato and fennel into
a roasting tin. Add the oil and sprinkle with salt and
pepper. Toss to coat, then roast in a preheated oven at
200°C (400°F) Gas 6 for 45 minutes, checking after
30 minutes that the vegetables are cooking evenly and
turning them if needed. Add the chickpeas and roast for
a further 5–10 minutes until all the vegetables are
browned and tender.

To make the tomato sauce, heat the oil in a saucepan.
Add the onion, celery, leek and garlic and sauté for
5 minutes until soft. Add the tomatoes, tomato purée
and red wine. Simmer gently for 30 minutes, adding
a little more red wine if the sauce becomes too thick.
Using a hand-held stick blender, process until smooth.
Add salt and pepper to taste, pour over the roasted
vegetables and serve with the Parmesan biscuits.

blackberry and apple pie

For the best pastry results, always use a metal pie dish: it will get hotter than ceramic and guarantees to cook the pastry until dry and crumbly rather than soggy.

PASTRY

350 g plain flour

200 g butter, cut into small pieces

80 g unrefined caster sugar, plus extra for sprinkling

3–4 egg yolks

milk, for brushing

FILLING

800 g cooking apples, such as Bramley, cored, peeled and sliced

400 g blackberries

100 g unrefined caster sugar

real custard (below, right), to serve

a metal pie dish, 25 cm diameter, lightly buttered

serves 4

Put the flour and butter into a food processor and process until the mixture looks like breadcrumbs. Add the sugar and process briefly. With the machine running, gradually add 3 egg yolks until the mixture comes together to form a ball. (Add the extra egg yolk if it is too dry.) Transfer the pastry to a lightly floured surface and knead very gently with your hands until smooth. Divide in half, wrap each piece in clingfilm and chill for 40 minutes.

Remove 1 piece of chilled pastry from the refrigerator and roll out until just larger than the pie dish. Put the rolled pastry into the pie dish, pressing the base and rim gently to push out any air bubbles. Layer the apple slices, blackberries and sugar over the pastry, piling the fruit high, then brush milk over the pastry rim.

Roll out the remaining pastry to just bigger than the dish and drape it over the fruit, taking care not to stretch it. Trim the excess pastry away from the edge and then go around the rim of the pie, pinching the pastry together with your fingers to seal. Using a small, sharp knife, cut a vent in the middle of the pie to let the steam escape.

Brush the pastry all over with milk and sprinkle generously with sugar. Cook in a preheated oven at 220°C (425°F) Gas 7 for 30 minutes, then reduce to 180°C (350°F) Gas 4 and cook for another 30 minutes until golden. Serve hot with custard.

real custard

It takes a little time and patience, and a very gentle heat, to make this custard so rich and glossy – but it's worth it. Don't try to hurry, or the eggs will scramble.

2 vanilla pods

350 ml milk

250 ml double cream

75 g unrefined caster sugar

4 large egg yolks

serves 4

Split the vanilla pods in half lengthways and scrape out the seeds. Put the milk, cream, sugar and vanilla seeds into a saucepan and heat gently until just before boiling point, then reduce the heat to low. Put the egg yolks into a bowl and whisk until frothy. Add a little of the hot milk mixture to the eggs and whisk again. Pour the egg yolk mixture into the saucepan and whisk again. Cook over very low heat, stirring constantly with a wooden spoon, until the custard thickens, about 6 minutes. Serve.

weekend dining

the scene

Weekend dining is always special to me. Weekdays are often rushed, but at last, at the weekend, there's time for cooking at home with ease. I love being in the kitchen, slowly preparing a great meal, the radio on, maybe glancing through the newspaper, catching up on a few small kitchen tasks. As the food is roasted, it gradually fills the house with warmth and delicious aromas.

the style

Happy chaos catering for all ages and needs, so let your children set the table and gather all that's needed. There is something traditional about a roast lunch, so it's a good time to wheel out bone-handled cutlery and family heirloom china.

sage and stilton flatbread

Make this as a starter to serve with drinks when your friends and family arrive. If Stilton is not your favourite cheese, try using another blue cheese such as Roquefort or Gorgonzola, brie or a hard cheese such as mature Cheddar.

500 g plain flour

1 teaspoon baking powder

225 ml Greek yoghurt

100 g butter, melted

2 eggs, beaten

3 tablespoons chopped fresh sage

100 g Stilton cheese, crumbled

a baking sheet, lightly oiled

serves 8

Sift the flour and baking powder into a bowl and make a well in the middle. Put the yoghurt, melted butter, eggs and sage into a separate bowl and mix. Pour the mixture into the well in the flour and stir with a wooden spoon until well blended.

Knead the dough into a ball, put onto the prepared baking sheet and roll out to a 30 cm disc. Cook in a preheated oven at 180°C (350°F) Gas 4 for 20 minutes. Remove, crumble the Stilton over the top and return to the oven for a further 10 minutes. Remove and let cool a little before removing from the dish. Transfer to a large chopping board, cut into wedges and serve.

THE MENU
FOR 8 PEOPLE

Sage and Stilton Flatbread

Roast Rib of Beef with Horseradish Yorkshire Puddings

Roast Potatoes and Parsnips

Carrot and Spinach Butter Mash

Vin Santo Trifle

TO DRINK

Syrah (Shiraz), Merlot, Cabernet Sauvignon

THE WORK PLAN

the day before

- Make the trifle, cover and chill.

on the day

- Preheat the oven until hot.
- Prepare the beef, calculate the cooking time and put into the preheated oven.
- Make the flatbread and serve with pre-lunch drinks.
- Par-boil the potatoes and transfer to the oven to roast. Par-boil the parsnips (reserving the water), drain and set aside.
- Cook the carrots (reserving the water), drain and keep them warm in the oven.
- Add the parsnips to the potatoes, to roast.
- Prepare and cook the Yorkshire puddings.
- Remove the beef from the oven and keep it warm while you make the gravy and cook the Yorkshire puddings.
- Mash the carrots, add the spinach and cook while someone carves the beef.

roast rib of beef

When winter closes in, I always want to cook this meal, perfect for a large, happy gathering around a table ringing with laughter and good stories. To make carving easier, ask the butcher to debone and roll the beef, but make sure you get the bones as well and roast them with the meat. They add to the flavour of the gravy (very important – without good gravy it's not a true roast!)

3-bone rib of beef, about 3 kg

2 tablespoons plain flour

2 teaspoons English mustard powder

2 teaspoons freshly ground black pepper

1 tablespoon oil

GRAVY

1 tablespoon plain flour

reserved cooking water from the parsnips and carrots

a splash of Worcestershire sauce

salt and freshly ground black pepper

serves 8

Put the flour, mustard powder and pepper into a bowl, mix briefly, then rub the rib of beef all over with the mixture. Heat the oil in a large roasting tin, add the beef, then put into a preheated oven at 200°C (400°F) Gas 6. After 20 minutes reduce the heat to 180°C (350°F) Gas 4 and cook for a further 20 minutes per 500 g for rare, 25 minutes per 500 g for medium and 30 minutes per 500 g for well done. Remove the beef from the oven and let rest for 20 minutes, while you make the Yorkshire puddings (right).

Remove the beef from the roasting tin and drain off the excess oil. To make the gravy, add the flour to the tin and stir to form a paste. Put on top of the stove over high heat and gradually add the vegetable water, stirring and scraping up all the residue from the roasting tin, until you have a good gravy consistency. Bring to the boil and add salt, pepper and a splash of Worcestershire sauce. Pour into a jug and keep it warm until needed.

horseradish yorkshire puddings

The trick for Yorkshire puddings is to have the oven hot and to preheat the oil in the tin. Cook them only when everyone is ready and everything is organized and under control in the kitchen – if they are not eaten at once, they will deflate and lose their crunch!

75 g plain flour

1 egg

75 ml milk

1 teaspoon grated fresh horseradish

50 g lard or beef dripping

sea salt and freshly ground black pepper

a 12-hole muffin tin

serves 8

Sift the flour into a bowl and make a well in the middle. Put the egg, milk, horseradish and 50 ml water into a separate bowl, add a pinch of salt and pepper and mix. Slowly pour the mixture into the well in the flour, beating with electric beaters or a wooden spoon until you have a smooth batter.

While the beef is resting out of the oven, increase the oven temperature to 220°C (425°F) Gas 7. Divide the lard between 8 of the muffin holes and heat the tin in the oven for 10 minutes. Remove and fill the 8 holes with batter. Cook at the top of the oven for 8–10 minutes until puffed and golden.

roast potatoes and parsnips

When cooking roast potatoes, the oven should be very hot – hotter than for the beef. If you have a double oven, this is no problem, as the meat can be in one and the potatoes in another, but with a single oven you have to play around with the temperature and the position of the food. Increase the oven temperature, and cook the roast rib at the bottom of the oven and the potatoes at the top. You may need to reduce the cooking time for the beef, or remove it from the oven for 20 minutes before it is finished, keep it warm and then return and continue to cook. It sounds tricky but really it's not – I call it oven juggling!

500 g potatoes, cut into equal pieces
500 g parsnips, cut into equal pieces
6 tablespoons olive oil
sea salt

serves 8

Cook the potatoes in a saucepan of boiling, salted water for 12 minutes, drain well and return them to the pan. Put over low heat for 2 minutes, to steam off the excess moisture. Cover with a lid and shake the pan vigorously a few times, to give the potatoes a floury coating. Add 4 tablespoons of the oil and coat well.

Cook the parsnips in a saucepan of boiling salted water for 8 minutes, then drain well, reserving the cooking water for the gravy. Add the remaining 2 tablespoons oil to the parsnips and shake to coat.

Put the potatoes into a large roasting tin and cook in a preheated oven at 220°C (425°F) Gas 7 for 20 minutes. Add the parsnips and return to the oven for a further 15 minutes until crunchy and golden.

vin santo trifle

This trifle is just delicious but, instead of custard, I use a mixture of cream and mascarpone. Go to an Italian deli for vin santo (a sweet wine) and biscotti (hard, almond-flavoured Italian biscuits). These are traditionally eaten dipped into the wine, but here make a splendid addition to trifle.

250 g Italian biscotti

100 ml vin santo

8 ripe figs, quartered lengthways

1 can pitted cherries, about 425 g

500 ml double cream

500 g mascarpone cheese

75 g unrefined caster sugar

50 g white chocolate

50 g flaked almonds

serves 8

Put the biscotti into a large serving bowl, preferably glass. Pour over the vin santo and arrange the figs and cherries on top. Put the cream into a bowl and whip lightly until soft peaks form. Add the mascarpone and sugar and continue whisking until stiff. Spoon the cream and mascarpone mixture over the fruit, then sprinkle with almonds. Using a vegetable peeler (or an Italian truffle slicer if you have one), make curls with the white chocolate and sprinkle over the trifle. Chill until needed.

carrot and spinach butter mash

400 g carrots, chopped

75 g butter

300 g spinach, chopped

sea salt and freshly ground black pepper

serves 8

Cook the carrots in a saucepan of boiling, salted water for 30 minutes, or until tender. Drain well, reserving the cooking water for the gravy. Return the carrots to the pan and put over low heat. Steam off the excess water, stirring frequently, for 2 minutes. Remove from the heat, add the butter, salt and pepper and mash well. Add the spinach and stir for 2 minutes, until wilted.

THE MENU

FOR 6 PEOPLE

Filo Spinach and Ricotta Pastries

Slow-roasted Tomatoes

Daube of Beef

or

Fish and Spring Greens Pie

Panettone Bread and Butter Pudding with Plums

TO DRINK

Merlot for the Beef, Zinfandel or Gamay for the Fish Pie

THE WORK PLAN

two days before

- Marinate the beef, cover and chill overnight.

the day before

- Cook the daube of beef. Remove from the oven, let cool, then chill overnight.

on the day

- Prepare but do not cook the filo pastries, put onto the baking sheet, cover and chill.
- Prepare but do not cook the fish pie, cover in clingfilm and chill.
- Prepare but do not cook the bread and butter pudding, cover and chill.

just before serving

- Cook the filo pastries.
- Reheat the daube of beef or cook the fish pie.
- Cook the bread and butter pudding.
- Cook pasta or potatoes to serve with the beef.

dinner in advance

the scene

We all lead busy lives, and sometimes we invite friends over and then find we are snowed under with work – we've all been there! But this is a totally prepare-in-advance menu with just the simplest last-minute cooking, so you can rush home late and still serve a stunning meal.

the style

A setting to match the cook – calm and unflustered. As time is short, you can set the table the night before, or even in the morning, but really it should be simple and homely. Your guests should be welcomed by the sight of a serene cook and table, then a happy, easy meal will follow naturally.

filo spinach and ricotta pastries

These delicious little parcels of spinach and creamy ricotta encased in crisp filo pastry are originally from Morocco, but these days they can be found all around the Mediterranean, with countless variations.

350 g baby spinach, washed and dried

150 g filo pastry

50 g butter, melted

250 g fresh ricotta cheese

50 g pine nuts, toasted in a dry frying pan

sea salt and freshly ground black pepper

serves 6

Put the spinach into a large saucepan over medium heat. Cook, stirring, until all the leaves have wilted, about 5 minutes. Transfer to a large colander and let cool, while the excess liquid drips out.

Put a tea towel onto a clean work surface and put a sheet of filo on top. Brush with melted butter and layer 3 more of the sheets on top, brushing each with butter. Put the ricotta, pine nuts, cooled spinach, salt and pepper into a bowl and mix. Spread the mixture over the filo, leaving a 5 cm border all around.

Starting with the long side, roll up the filo into a log shape, using the cloth to help you roll. Lightly twist the ends to enclose. Brush all over with butter, transfer to a baking sheet and cook in a preheated oven at 180°C (350°F) Gas 4 for 30 minutes until golden. Slice and serve with the slow-roasted tomatoes.

slow-roasted tomatoes

6 tomatoes, halved crossways

serves 6

Put the tomato halves, skin side down, into an oven dish, spacing them so that they do not touch. Cook in a preheated oven at 120°C (250°F) Gas 1/2 for 2 hours. Serve with the filo pastries.

daube of beef

This dish must be made in advance in order for the flavours to develop and the sauce to taste rich and delicious. If you are reheating it from cold, put into a preheated oven at 180°C (350°F) Gas 4 for 35 minutes.

1.75 kg rump of beef

1 bottle white wine, 750 ml

2 bay leaves

4 tablespoons olive oil

2 onions, sliced

2 garlic cloves, crushed and chopped

3 tablespoons plain flour, plus extra for dusting

1 tablespoon drained capers

100 g pitted black olives

1 can chopped tomatoes, 410 g

grated zest of 1/2 orange

200 g baby carrots

125 g button mushrooms

a large bunch of flat leaf parsley, chopped

sea salt and freshly ground black pepper

serves 6

Put the beef, wine, bay leaves, salt and pepper into a large bowl, cover and chill for 24 hours, turning the beef in its marinade from time to time.

Drain the beef, reserving the marinade, and pat dry with kitchen paper. Heat 2 tablespoons of the oil in a large flameproof casserole, add the onions and garlic and cook gently for 3 minutes. Sprinkle with the flour and stir. Add the marinade liquid a little at a time, stirring constantly. Add the capers, olives, tomatoes and orange zest and simmer while you prepare the beef.

Put the remaining olive oil into a frying pan and heat until hot. Dust the beef in flour and add to the frying pan. Fry until brown on all sides, then transfer to the casserole. Put a few tablespoons of juice from the casserole back into the frying pan and stir to scrape up any meaty bits. Add the juice and bits back to the casserole.

Cover with a lid, transfer to a preheated oven at 140°C (275°F) Gas 1 and cook for 2 hours. Remove from the oven and add the carrots and mushrooms. Return the casserole to the oven and cook for another hour.

Remove the beef to a board, slice thickly and serve on heated dinner plates. Stir the chopped parsley into the sauce and spoon the sauce and vegetables over the beef. Serve with egg noodle pasta, tossed in parsley and butter, or with boiled potatoes.

Nothing beats a good daube of beef, and this one is perfect, because it's mine! The meat is tender, the juices rich and vegetables succulent.

fish and spring greens pie

Everyone loves a creamy fish pie, packed with goodness.

500 g white fish fillet, such as cod, haddock or whiting

500 g trout fillet

200 g uncooked peeled prawns

100 g scallops

300 g spring greens or Savoy cabbage, coarsely chopped

1 kg potatoes, cut into equal pieces

50 g butter

100 ml milk

sea salt and freshly ground black pepper

SAUCE

500 ml milk

100 g butter

50 g plain flour

100 g Cheddar cheese, grated

sea salt and freshly ground black pepper

serves 6

Dry the fish and seafood thoroughly with kitchen paper. Arrange the spring greens in a large ovenproof dish and put the fish and seafood on top.

Cook the potatoes in a saucepan of boiling, salted water for 20 minutes, or until tender when pierced with a knife. Drain and return to the pan. Mash well, then add the butter, milk and salt and pepper to taste. Beat well with a wooden spoon, then set aside until needed.

To make the sauce, put the milk into a small saucepan and heat gently until warm. Melt the butter in a separate saucepan and add the flour. Remove from the heat, stir, return to the heat, then add a little of the warm milk. Stir well, then gradually stir in the remaining warm milk until the sauce is smooth. Add the cheese, salt and pepper, then pour over the fish.

Spoon the mashed potatoes evenly over the top, giving it a scalloped effect. If you want a more traditional look, run a fork over the surface of the potato. Transfer to a preheated oven at 200°C (400°F) Gas 6 and bake for 20 minutes, then reduce to 160°C (325°F) Gas 3 and cook for a further 25 minutes.

One of my comfort foods is fish pie. The velvety sauce, the creamy mashed potato – it's a dish I revisit time and again.

panettone bread and butter pudding with plums

Traditional bread and butter pudding, with creamy custard and plump raisins, is wonderful. I think it's even better with rich Italian panettone and juicy blush plums.

6 slices panettone or other sweet bread, spread with butter

6 ripe plums, halved, pitted and sliced

300 ml milk

100 ml double cream

50 g unrefined caster sugar

3 eggs

a baking dish, enamel if possible, buttered

serves 6

Cut the slices of buttered panettone in half and put a few slices of plum on top. Arrange in an overlapping layer in the baking dish.

Put the milk, cream, sugar and eggs into a bowl and whisk. Pour the mixture over the panettone and plums. Chop any remaining plum slices into small pieces and sprinkle over the top. Set aside for 1 hour to let the panettone soak up the creamy liquid.

Cook in a preheated oven at 180°C (350°F) Gas 4 for about 35 minutes. Serve warm.

THE WORK PLAN

the day before

- Make the orange and lemon bake, cover and store in a cool place.
- Prepare the pork fillet, cover and chill.

on the day

- Make the lime and soy dressing for the tuna, cover and chill.
- Roast the peppers and cook the lentils.
- Make the minted yoghurt.
- Make the spring onion dressing for the pork, cover and chill.
- Cook the potatoes and beans, drain and set aside.

just before serving

- Cook the pork.
- Assemble the salad.
- Prepare the chicory and watercress for the salad.
- Sear the tuna.

summer sundown

the scene

At the end of a hot summer's day, relax in the garden and enjoy this fresh and tangy menu full of seasonal produce. Outdoor eating is a real treat for all, so if you have a garden or a terrace, use it.

the style

Pretty and romantic, just keep it easy and calm so that it doesn't detract from the beauty of your surroundings. Use soft colours with informal china to create a warm and relaxed table so you can enjoy the food and the view.

seared tuna salad with lime and soy dressing

Tuna is such a popular fish today and with the availability of quality fresh tuna, it is a joy to cook and eat.

300 g fresh tuna steak

grated zest and freshly squeezed juice of 2 limes, plus extra wedges, to serve

1 chilli, finely chopped

100 ml light soy sauce

2 kaffir lime leaves, finely sliced

1 stalk of lemongrass, very finely sliced

3 tablespoons olive oil

3 heads of chicory, leaves separated

2 bunches of watercress

salt and freshly ground black pepper

serves 8

Heat a stove-top grill pan until very hot, then add the tuna steak. Cook for 2–3 minutes on each side. Don't move it around before this or it will not have formed a good crust and will break up. Remove to a carving board and let rest.

To make the dressing, put the lime zest and juice into a bowl. Add the chilli, soy sauce, lime leaves, lemongrass, oil and salt and pepper to taste. Arrange the chicory on serving plates. Cut the tuna crossways into fine slices and arrange on top of the salad. Add the watercress and wedges of lime, spoon the dressing over the top and serve.

If Puy lentils are not available, use brown lentils instead – they have a delicious, earthy flavour.

sage-stuffed pork fillet with puy lentils and spring onion dressing

This meal would be fit to serve in many restaurants and yet is very simple. Fillet of pork is a much under-used cut, but it is so quick and easy to cook. People seem to worry a great deal about pork being undercooked or tough, but follow the instructions and it will always be cooked through and moist.

2 pork fillets, about 375 g each

leaves from a large bunch of sage

8 thin slices Parma ham

250 g Puy lentils

6 spring onions, sliced

3 tablespoons olive oil

1 tablespoon red wine

100 ml sour cream

500 g roasted red peppers in a jar, drained and cut into strips

a bunch of chives, chopped

sea salt and freshly ground black pepper

serves 8

Trim the pork fillets of any excess fat and, using a long, thin knife, pierce each fillet lengthways through the middle. Push the sage leaves into the slit and, using the handle of a wooden spoon, push them further along the slit. Sprinkle the filets with salt and pepper, then wrap each one in 4 slices of Parma ham. Brush a roasting tin with oil, add the wrapped filets and cook in a preheated oven at 180°C (350°F) Gas 4 for 35 minutes. Remove, let rest for 5 minutes, then cut into 3 cm thick slices.

Meanwhile, cook the lentils in simmering water for 20 minutes until tender, then drain. Put the spring onions into a bowl, add the oil, wine and sour cream and mix. Add the peppers to the drained lentils and spoon onto serving plates. Top with the pork slices, spring onion dressing and chives, then serve.

new potato, garden pea and bean salad

A wonderful combination of summer ingredients, bursting with fresh vegetable flavours. If fresh peas aren't available, use frozen instead.

1.2 kg new potatoes

300 g shelled peas

300 g flat beans, trimmed

2 garlic cloves, crushed and chopped

6 tablespoons olive oil

2 tablespoons Dijon mustard

freshly squeezed juice of 1 lemon

sea salt and freshly ground black pepper

leaves from a bunch of flat leaf parsley, to serve

serves 8

Cook the potatoes in boiling, salted water for 20 minutes or until tender, then drain and set aside. Cook the peas and flat beans together in boiling, salted water for 4 minutes. Drain and refresh in changes of cold water until cool, then drain again.

Put the garlic into a small bowl and add the oil, mustard, lemon juice and salt and pepper to taste. Cut the potatoes in half and put into a large bowl. Add the peas and beans and mix. Just before serving, add the dressing, toss well to coat and sprinkle with parsley.

4 eggs

100 g unrefined
caster sugar

100 g desiccated coconut

50 g softened butter

100 g ground almonds

grated zest and freshly
squeezed juice of
2 unwaxed lemons

grated zest and juice of
2 oranges

100 ml milk

50 g self-raising flour

MINTED YOGHURT

200 ml Greek yoghurt

a bunch of mint, finely chopped

*a pie dish, 18 cm diameter,
buttered*

serves 8

orange and lemon bake with minted yoghurt

This is a mixture of things that I love – sponge pudding, coconut, ground almonds and citrus fruits.

To make the bake, put the eggs, sugar, coconut, butter, ground almonds, lemon and orange zest and juice, milk and self-raising flour into a food processor and process for 1 minute until blended. Transfer the mixture to the buttered dish and bake in a preheated oven at 180°C (350°F) Gas 4 for 45 minutes until golden brown. Remove from the oven and let cool.

Put the yoghurt into a bowl and add the mint. Mix well and serve spooned over the bake.

country chicken

If you don't fancy cutting up a whole chicken, ask the butcher to do it for you, or simply buy chicken pieces.

Put the chicken pieces into a bowl and add the shallots, bay leaves, bacon, oil, salt and pepper. Mix well, transfer to a roasting tin and cook in a preheated oven at 180°C (350°F) Gas 4 for 30 minutes.

Put the mustard into a small bowl, then stir in the tarragon and wine. Remove the chicken from the oven and pour off any excess fat. Pour the mustard and tarragon mixture over the chicken and return it to the oven for a further 10 minutes. Serve with the pasta ribbons.

1 chicken, about 2 kg,
cut into 8 pieces

8 shallots

5 bay leaves

250 g bacon, chopped

2 tablespoons olive oil

1½ tablespoons wholegrain mustard

a bunch of tarragon, coarsely chopped

100 ml white wine

sea salt and freshly ground black pepper

serves 4

pasta ribbons with parsley

I love pappardelle pasta. Because of its extra width, whatever sauce you add, it will cling more easily and thus give more flavour.

Cook the pasta in a large saucepan of boiling, salted water until *al dente*, or according to the instructions on the packet.

Drain the pasta well and return it to the pan, off the heat. Add the parsley, garlic, oil, lemon juice and salt and pepper to taste. Toss well, then serve.

400 g dried pappardelle pasta

a bunch of flat leaf parsley, coarsely chopped

1 garlic clove, finely chopped

4 tablespoons olive oil

freshly squeezed juice of ½ lemon

sea salt and freshly ground black pepper

serves 4

THE WORK PLAN

the day before

- Make the lemon polenta cake, let cool, then cover and store at room temperature. If serving hot, put the dish into a tray of water (to stop it drying out) and transfer to a preheated oven for 10 minutes at 150°C (300°F) Gas 2. Alternatively, reheat in the microwave for 6–7 minutes on MED.
- Cut the chicken into pieces if whole and put into a bowl with the marinade ingredients. Cover and chill overnight.

just before serving

- Transfer the chicken to the roasting tin and put into the oven to cook.
- Make the tarragon and mustard mixture for the chicken.
- Prepare and cook the peppers.
- Cook the pasta, chop the parsley and garlic.

lemon polenta cake with pouring cream

Remove the butter from the refrigerator 30 minutes before starting this recipe: when softer, it's easier to mix.

250 g butter, cut into pieces
250 g unrefined caster sugar
4 eggs
3 unwaxed lemons
125 g polenta
125 g self-raising flour
300 ml single cream, to serve

an ovenproof dish, 20 cm diameter, lightly buttered

serves 4

Put the butter into a mixing bowl, add the sugar and beat until creamy and smooth. Beat in the eggs one at a time (the mixture may separate, but will come back together when the flour is added).

Grate the zest and squeeze the juice from 2½ of the lemons. Slice the remaining lemon half and set aside. Add the lemon zest and juice to the cake mixture and mix well. Add the polenta and flour, fold in until evenly blended, then spoon into the buttered dish. Arrange the reserved lemon slices around the middle of the cake.

Bake in a preheated oven at 130°C (350°F) Gas 4 for 25 minutes. Reduce to 160°C (325°F) Gas 3 and cook for a further 10 minutes, until it is coming away from the edges of the dish and a knife inserted in the centre comes out clean. Serve hot or at room temperature, with a jug of cream.

prawn noodle broth

If, like me, you love a fiery heat, leave the seeds in the chillies.

1 tablespoon vegetable oil

1 onion, sliced

10 cm fresh ginger or galangal, peeled and sliced

2 garlic cloves, sliced

2 red chillies, deseeded (optional) and sliced

600 g uncooked peeled tiger prawns

2 litres vegetable stock

600 g fresh udon noodles

a bunch of Thai basil, coarsely chopped

a bunch of coriander, coarsely chopped

serves 8

Heat the oil in a saucepan and add the onion, ginger or galangal, garlic and chillies. Stir well and cook for 5 minutes over low heat. Add the prawns and cook for a further 2 minutes, then add the stock. Bring to the boil, add the noodles and cook for a further 2 minutes. Stir the Thai basil and coriander into the broth and serve.

fab fish lunch

the scene

The beauty of fish calls for simplicity, but these dishes can all be dressed up or down to suit any occasion.

the style

Serve from big vessels to enhance that look of the sea's bounty. Let everyone help themselves to more whenever they feel like it.

THE WORK PLAN

the day before

- Make the chowder, but don't add the cream and herbs. Cover and chill.
- Prepare the smoking tin, fillet the trout and wrap it in prosciutto.
- Roll, tie and smoke the trout. Let cool, cover and chill.
- Make the lime mousse and lemon sauce.

on the day

- Make the prawn noodle broth, but don't add the prawns or noodles.
- Make the fish stew up to the point of adding herbs.

just before serving

- Make the cucumber salad. Slice the trout and cook on the grill pan.
- Finish all the above dishes to serve.

THE MENU

SERVES 8

Prawn Noodle Broth

Smoked Haddock Chowder

Tea-smoked Trout with Cucumber Salad

Easy Fish Stew

Lime Mousse with Lemon Sauce

TO DRINK

Gewüztraminer, Pinot Grigio, Semillon

smoked haddock chowder

This classic recipe is just perfect for damp and cold days – it will warm and satisfy everyone. In the US, they serve it with crumbled crackers added at the table, but I prefer to serve it with thickly sliced mixed-grain bread

Heat the butter in a large saucepan. Add the leeks and bacon and cook for 5 minutes, but do not brown. Add the fish stock and bring to a simmer. Add the sweetcorn, potatoes and fish and cook for 10 minutes. Add salt and pepper to taste and bring to a gentle boil. Just before serving, add the parsley, chives and cream. Serve with thick slices of warm bread.

50 g butter

2 leeks, finely sliced

100 g smoked bacon, chopped

600 ml fish stock

125 g canned sweetcorn, drained and rinsed

100 g potatoes, cut into small cubes

300 g fillet undyed smoked haddock, skinned

1 tablespoon chopped, fresh flat leaf parsley

1 tablespoon chopped chives

100 ml double cream

sea salt and freshly ground black pepper

serves 8

tea-smoked trout with cucumber salad

This takes a little time, but for that special occasion is well worth it, as the flavour is so different. I love the way the fillets are rolled together, then tied and cut to give you a boneless slice of fish. An unusual treat for the taste buds.

75 g oak wood shavings

1 tablespoon jasmine tea

1 whole trout, about 2 kg, filleted and skinned

12 slices prosciutto

2 tablespoons sesame oil

CUCUMBER SALAD

2 cucumbers, peeled and halved lengthways

grated zest and freshly squeezed juice of 2 limes

sea salt and freshly ground black pepper

an old roasting tin, lined with foil

a wire rack

serves 8

Put the wood shavings and tea into the lined roasting tin and mix well. Put a wire rack that fits the tin on top.

Put both trout fillets onto a cutting board, one on top of the other, top to tail. Shape with your hands into a long sausage. Wrap the prosciutto around the fillets, overlapping slightly, to cover completely. Tie pieces of kitchen string around the trout at 5 cm intervals to secure, then cut into 8 thick slices. Rub the cut surfaces with sesame oil and transfer to the wire rack set over the roasting tin.

Completely cover the top of the tin with foil, making sure that it is sealed all the way around the edge to stop any smoke escaping. Put the tin over high heat for 10 minutes, moving it around from time to time, to ensure even smoking. Remove from the heat and let cool, covered, for 20 minutes.

To make the cucumber salad, scoop out the seeds from the peeled cucumber halves and discard. Finely slice the cucumber and put into a bowl. Add the lime zest and juice and salt and pepper to taste.

Heat a stove-top grill pan or a non-stick frying pan until hot, add the smoked trout steaks and cook for 3 minutes on each side. They should be brown and slightly crunchy on the outside. Remove and discard the string and serve the fish with the cucumber salad.

easy fish stew

I love fish stew, and this easy, stress-free recipe makes a fantastic meal (I have used it many times). Don't forget to provide a few empty dishes for discarded shells and some bowls of warm water for washing fingers.

5 tablespoons olive oil

3 garlic cloves, crushed and chopped

2 onions, chopped

2 leeks, trimmed and sliced

3 celery stalks, sliced

1 fennel bulb, trimmed and sliced

1 tablespoon plain flour

1 bay leaf

a sprig of thyme

a generous pinch of saffron threads

3 cans chopped tomatoes, 410 g each

2 litres fish stock

1 kg monkfish tail, cut into 8

500 g mussels in shells, scrubbed

8 scallops

8 uncooked prawns, shell on

a bunch of flat leaf parsley, chopped

sea salt and freshly ground black pepper

serves 8

Heat the oil in a large saucepan and add the garlic, onion, leeks, celery and fennel. Cook over low to medium heat for 10 minutes until soft. Sprinkle in the flour and stir well. Add the bay leaf, thyme, saffron, tomatoes, fish stock and salt and pepper to taste. Bring to the boil, then simmer for 25 minutes. Add the monkfish, mussels, scallops and prawns, cover with a lid and simmer very gently for 6 minutes. Remove from the heat and set aside, with the lid on, for 4 minutes. Add the parsley and serve with plenty of warm crusty bread.

lime mousse with lemon sauce

Make this mousse the night before as there is nothing worse than willing an unset mousse to set before serving.

	LEMON SAUCE
1 sachet powdered gelatine	4 tablespoons unrefined caster sugar
3 eggs separated	
75 g unrefined caster sugar	thinly pared zest and freshly squeezed juice of 2 unwaxed lemons
grated zest and freshly squeezed juice of 3 limes	
150 ml double cream	serves 8

Put 3 tablespoons hot water into a small bowl and sprinkle in the gelatine. Put the bowl into a warm oven or over a pan of simmering water about 10 minutes. When completely dissolved, remove to room temperature and let cool a little.

Put the egg yolks and sugar into a large bowl and beat with electric beaters until frothy and creamy. Add the lime zest and juice and beat well. Add the gelatine and beat again, then set aside for 5 minutes. Whisk the cream until soft peaks form, then fold into the lime mixture. Wash the beaters well and whisk the egg whites until stiff. Add to the lime mixture and whisk briefly. Spoon into individual pots or one serving bowl. Chill for at least 2 hours, or overnight.

To make the sauce, put the sugar, lemon juice and half the zest into a small saucepan and mix. Bring to the boil, then simmer for 1 minute. Remove from the heat and cool completely to a syrupy sauce. If it is a little too thick, stir in a small amount of water. Sprinkle the remaining lemon zest over the mousse and serve with the sauce.

parties & celebrations

This is red carpet dining. I love celebrating, and have been known to invent an occasion to be able to mark it with a special meal. Planning the reason, inviting friends, getting the look, choosing the menu and drinks, shopping, cooking and then eating, drinking and making merry. It's as happy and simple as that – so join me for a profusion of ideas and menus for that exciting celebration.

You don't have to be rich to be lavish and you can always cut corners. Don't invite too many people, especially if you don't have the space. Choose the menu according to your budget, and be prepared to adapt recipes (for example by using portobello mushrooms instead of porcini). Look out for wines as they appear on special offer and stock up.

Be organized. Make a list and work your way through it. Prepare as much of the food as possible in advance, set the table and chill the drinks several hours before your guests arrive. Set out a tray with coffee and chocolates and get pre-dinner drinks and glasses ready. Now go and have a bath, so that you look relaxed and happy to welcome your friends.

children's tea party

the scene

The birthday party is magical moment for every child, but it should also be fun for the parents. The most important thing to remember is not to over-cater – don't slave away in the kitchen, only to throw it all away because the children are just too excited to sit down and eat a healthy meal. They want treats – and at a party they should get them!

the style

Mini table and chairs with plates piled high. Use fun china for children with crazy designs, rather than plastic plates and cups. Balloons, of course!

cartwheel tortilla wraps

It's almost impossible to get children to eat something healthy at a birthday party, due to all the excitement, but don't give up. These wraps can be made the night before, then sliced just before the party, so removing some of the stress from Mum!

3 flour tortillas

butter, for spreading

3 tablespoons cream cheese

1 large carrot, grated

serves 12

Put each tortilla flat onto a piece of clingfilm, spread with butter and cream cheese, sprinkle with carrot and roll up tightly, using the clingfilm to help, and twisting the clingfilm at either end. Chill for 2 hours to set, then cut into slices. Remove the clingfilm and serve.

star and heart sandwiches

Choose a variety of breads – wholegrain, brown, rye and white. Any shapes can be used, so let your artistic side run wild.

24 slices bread, a mixture of brown and white, buttered

FILLINGS:

marmite and cream cheese, ham and mayonnaise, pesto, hoummus, sliced avocado

star- and heart-shaped pastry cutters

serves 12

Arrange half the buttered bread slices on a work surface and top with a selection of fillings. Put the remaining bread slices on top and cut out shaped sandwiches with the star and heart cutters.

THE MENU

FOR 12 CHILDREN

Cartwheel Tortilla Wraps

Star and Heart Sandwiches

Cheese Number Puffs

Jam Tarts

Chocolate-dipped Strawberries

Boys' and Girls' Meringues

Fruit Stars and Hearts

Bedazzled Fairy Cake Mountain

cheese number puffs

You can use other hard cheeses, such as Cheddar, Emmental or Gruyère, instead of Parmesan.

500 g puff pastry

1 egg, beaten

125 g Parmesan cheese, grated

number-shaped pastry cutters

a baking sheet, lightly greased

serves 12

Roll out the pastry on a lightly floured surface until very thin. Brush all over with the beaten egg and sprinkle evenly with Parmesan. Using the number pastry cutters, stamp out numbers and transfer them carefully to the baking sheet. Cook in a preheated oven at 180°C (350°F) Gas 4 for 20 minutes until puffed and golden.

jam tarts

If you have time, make the pastry yourself and get the children to help. They love it and they pick it up so quickly – a little patience goes a long way with pastry rolling. If time is short, buy shortcrust pastry. Make sure you let the tarts cool properly before eating, as jam can get very hot.

200 g plain flour	12-hole tart tin, buttered
100 g butter, cut into pieces	8 cm biscuit cutter
2 eggs, beaten	
200 g fruit jam	serves 12
caster sugar, for sprinkling	

Put the flour into a mixing bowl and add the butter. Using your fingertips, rub the butter into the flour until the mixture looks like breadcrumbs. Gradually add the eggs, using a round-bladed knife to cut the mixture, until it forms a ball. Using your hands, gently knead it in the bowl until the mixture is even. Cover with clingfilm and chill for 20 minutes.

Transfer the pastry to a lightly floured, cool surface and roll out to a large rectangle. Using the pastry cutters, stamp out 12 rounds and use to line the holes in the tart tin. Put a teaspoon of jam into each tart and sprinkle with a little sugar. Don't use too much jam, or it will bubble over and stick.

Bake the tarts in a preheated oven at 180°C (350°F) Gas 4 for 20 minutes, then reduce to 150°C (300°F) Gas 2 and bake for a further 10 minutes until the pastry is golden. If the tarts are a little low on jam, gently heat the remaining jam in a small saucepan. When soft, add a little extra to each tart. Remove from the tin and let cool.

chocolate-dipped strawberries

We all know that children love chocolate – but I find I can balance that by combining it with fruit, such as these beautiful strawberries. Any variety of fruits can be dipped but the colour of strawberries always looks so good.

100 g dark chocolate	bakewell paper
100 g white chocolate	12 wooden skewers
12 large strawberries	serves 12

Put the chocolate into 2 separate bowls and set the bowls over 2 saucepans of simmering water. When melted, dip the pointed end of each strawberry into one of the chocolates and transfer to the sheet of bakewell paper. When set, slide each strawberry onto a skewer and serve.

boys' and girls' meringues

I sometimes call these baby meringues 'fairies' wishes'. Add a little colour to them so they will suit the little pixies at your birthday table!

2 egg whites	a large baking sheet, lined with bakewell paper
125 g unrefined caster sugar	
red food colouring	serves 12
blue food colouring	

Put the egg whites into a clean bowl and whisk until stiff. Add half the sugar and continue whisking until stiff and shiny. Remove half the mixture to a second bowl.

Add a drop of red food colouring and half the remaining sugar to the first bowl, whisk and adjust the colouring if you want it stronger. Add a drop of blue food colouring to the second bowl and whisk in the remaining sugar.

Using a teaspoon, spoon out onto the prepared baking sheet and cook in a preheated oven at 140°C (275°F) Gas 1 for 2 hours.

THE WORK PLAN

up to a week before

- Make the meringues up to a week in advance and store in a sealed plastic bag (use a straw to suck out all the excess air).
- Bake the cakes and let cool.

the day before

- Assemble, ice and decorate the cake – then hide it!
- Make the cheese number puffs and store in an airtight container.
- Make the tortilla cartwheels, wrap in clingfilm and chill.
- Bake the jam tarts and store in an airtight container.

on the day

- Make the sandwiches (except avocado), wrap and chill.
- Dip the strawberries in chocolate and put onto skewers.

just before serving

- Stamp out the fruit shapes.
- Slice the tortilla cartwheels.
- Make the avocado sandwiches, if using.
- Unwrap and set out the food.

fruit stars and hearts

favourite fruits such as melon, pineapple, kiwifruit, mango or banana

orange or lemon juice, for brushing

small shaped cutters

serves 12

Cut the fruit into 1 cm thick slices. Use the cutters to stamp out shapes. If using apple, pear or banana, brush them with the juice to prevent them turning brown.

bedazzled fairy cake mountain

This is a very simple way to make this magic mountain cake – it is just a stack of four cakes in decreasing sizes, all sandwiched together, iced and topped with favourite sweets or chocolate curls. Instead of candles, try using sparklers or call it the mud mountain and cover with chocolate and dark green sweets.

750 g butter

750 g unrefined caster sugar

12 eggs

750 g self-raising flour

3 non-stick cake tins, about 15, 20 and 25 cm diameter, buttered, plus one paper muffin case

1 tartlet tin

serves 12

Make the cakes in 2 batches. Put 300 g of the butter and 300 g of the caster sugar into a bowl and cream together until light and fluffy. Add 5 of the eggs and whisk until mixed, then add 300 g of the flour and fold in until smooth. If it seems a little stiff, add a drop of milk.

Transfer to the largest cake tin and bake in a preheated oven at 180°C (350°F) Gas 4 for 30–40 minutes until golden, springy in the centre and just coming away from the edges of the tin.

Remove from the oven and let cool for 5 minutes, then remove from the tin and put onto a wire rack to cool.

Mix the remaining ingredients as before, filling the smaller 2 cake tins and the muffin case. Put the muffin case into an empty tart tin to help keep its shape. Put all 3 cakes into the preheated oven and bake for 25 minutes, checking as before to see if the cakes are cooked. Let cool completely before icing.

BUTTER ICING

250 g softened butter, cut into small pieces

500 g icing sugar

Put the butter and icing sugar into a bowl, add 2 tablespoons hot water and whisk until soft and creamy.

Put the largest cooled cake onto a wire rack and spread with butter icing. Put the middle sized cake on top and spread with butter icing. Top with the next cake and spread just the middle with butter icing. Peel the muffin paper away from the smallest cake and put on top in the middle.

TOP ICING

Either pick a colour and buy sweets that are all that colour, or have a mishmash of colours to create a jewel-encrusted cake. Choose very small sweets, such as jelly beans, Smarties®, dolly drops, chocolate shapes, tiny silver and gold drops and liquorice bootlaces.

500 g icing sugar

a big bag of sweets

food colouring or cocoa powder

chocolate

Put the icing sugar into a bowl. If using cocoa, mix 3 tablespoons with hot water, add to the icing sugar and mix. Otherwise just add colouring. Add water a little at a time and stir until smooth and blended. It should be thin enough to run down the cake, but still thick enough to cover it evenly. Pour over the cake, letting it cascade down and cover all of the cake.

While the icing is still wet, add the sweets, sticking them all over the cake, or grate chocolate over the cake. Hide and leave to set until needed for the lucky birthday child.

the scene

Girls can talk forever, and with this female-only gathering in the relaxed atmosphere of your own home, you can gossip away the afternoon without interruptions. Bliss!

the style

Make the setting indulgent to all things female. Surround yourself with the things you love – flowery tablecloth, plenty of flowers on the table, pretty glasses and cups, an elegant menu. Hide all the clocks so that time ticks by with no one noticing!

girls' reunion lunch

THE WORK PLAN

the day before

- Make the artichoke hoummus, cover and chill.
- Mix the nuts and spices ready for cooking, cover and store at room temperature.
- Make the pastry for the onion tart.
- Freeze the chocolate for the cakes.

on the day

- Bake the pastry for the tart and cook the onions.
- Prepare the salmon and wrap in prosciutto.
- Slice the courgettes, zest and juice the lemons.
- Assemble and cook the onion tart and make the salsa.
- Cook the nuts and toast the ciabatta.

just before serving

- Make and bake the cakes.
- Cook the salmon.
- Cook the pasta and courgette ribbons.

THE MENU
FOR 4 PEOPLE

Spiced Nuts

Artichoke Hoummus with Ciabatta

Onion Tart

Tomato Salsa

Roasted Salmon Wrapped in Prosciutto

Tossed Courgette Ribbons and Pasta

Marbled Chocolate Cakes

TO DRINK

Champagne, Chardonnay, Rosé

artichoke hoummus with ciabatta

You can make this dip the night before: just remember to remove it from the refrigerator a while before serving so the flavours can warm up. Serve with ciabatta bread, cheese straws, grissini (Italian breadsticks), pita, biscuits or other bread for dipping or spreading.

280 g artichoke hearts preserved in olive oil, drained

80 g drained, canned borlotti beans

sea salt and freshly ground black pepper

ciabatta bread, toasted, to serve

serves 4

Put the artichokes and beans into a food processor and blend until smooth. Transfer to a bowl, add salt and pepper to taste and serve with the toasted ciabatta and cheese straws or grissini.

spiced nuts

Take care that you let these cool before eating – the high oil content and density means they retain heat for longer than you might think.

1 teaspoon cumin seeds	100 g cashew nuts
1 teaspoon fennel seeds	100 g brazil nuts
	100 g almonds
1 teaspoon sweet smoked paprika	100 g peanuts
1 teaspoon flaked sea salt	100 g shelled pistachios
2 tablespoons olive oil	2 baking sheets
	serves 4

Crush the cumin and fennel seeds coarsely with a mortar and pestle. Transfer to a bowl and add the paprika, salt and oil. Mix well, then add all the nuts and mix again to coat. Spread in an even layer on 2 baking sheets and roast in a preheated oven at 180°C (350°F) Gas 4 for 10 minutes. Remove from the oven and turn with a spoon so they cook evenly. Return them to the oven and roast for a further 10 minutes. Remove and set aside to cool.

onion tart

Every good cook should be able to make a savoury tart, and this has to be one of the most delicious and popular. As it bakes, it fills your home with gorgeous baking aromas – your girlfriends will be impressed.

Sift the flour into a bowl and add the butter. Using your fingertips, rub the butter into the flour until the mixture looks like fine breadcrumbs. Add the beaten eggs and, using a round-bladed knife, cut through the mixture until it forms a ball. Knead lightly in the bowl with floured hands until evenly mixed, then cover and chill for 20 minutes.

Roll out the pastry on a lightly floured surface to a circle at least 5 cm bigger in diameter than the base of the tart tin. Drape the pastry over the rolling pin, carefully lift it up and lay it over the top of the tin. Gently press the pastry into the tin, making sure there are no air pockets, then use a sharp knife to trim off the excess pastry. Chill for 20 minutes.

To make the filling, melt the butter and oil in a saucepan, add the onions and cook over low heat for 30 minutes until soft and translucent, making sure they don't brown.

Line the pastry with baking parchment and baking beans or rice and bake in a preheated oven at 200°C (400°F) Gas 6 for 20 minutes. Remove the baking beans or rice and parchment, reduce to 160°C (325°F) Gas 3 and cook for a further 15 minutes until the pastry is set and lightly golden.

Put the eggs and cream into a large bowl and beat until mixed. Add the onions with salt and pepper to taste. Pour into the pastry case and bake in the oven for 25 minutes until set and golden. Serve warm or cold with tomato salsa.

PASTRY

250 g plain flour

175 g cold butter, cut into small pieces

2 eggs, beaten

FILLING

75 g butter

2 tablespoons olive oil

500 g onions, finely sliced

2 eggs

125 m single cream

sea salt and freshly ground black pepper

a tart tin, 20 cm diameter

baking parchment and baking beans or uncooked rice

serves 4

tomato salsa

4 tomatoes

3 spring onions, chopped

freshly squeezed juice of 1 lemon

a bunch of fresh flat leaf parsley, chopped

sea salt and freshly ground black pepper

serves 4

Cut a cross in the top of each tomato and put into a bowl. Cover with boiling water and leave for 30 seconds, then drain and peel. Cut each tomato into quarters, remove the core and seeds and chop the flesh. Put into a bowl and add the remaining ingredients. Mix and set aside for 2 hours. Serve with the tart.

When cooking for the girls, keep it light and fresh – except for pudding, when chocolate is a must!

roasted salmon wrapped in prosciutto

What makes this dish such a joy is that you will have no last-minute dramas with the fish falling to pieces, because the prosciutto not only adds flavour and crispness, it also parcels up the salmon and makes it easier to handle. Other fish such as trout, cod, halibut or monkfish are also good.

4 thin slices Fontina cheese, rind removed

4 salmon fillets, 175 g each, skinned

4 bay leaves

8 thin slices prosciutto

sea salt and freshly ground black pepper

a baking sheet, lightly oiled

serves 4

Trim the Fontina slices to fit on top of the salmon fillets. Put a bay leaf on top of each fillet, then a slice of the Fontina. Wrap 2 slices of prosciutto around each piece of salmon, so that it is completely covered.

Transfer to the baking sheet and cook in a preheated oven at 200°C (400°F) Gas 6 for 10–15 minutes, depending on the thickness of the salmon fillets.

tossed courgette ribbons and pasta

200 g dried pappardelle pasta

200 g courgettes, very finely sliced lengthways

finely grated zest and freshly squeezed juice of 1 unwaxed lemon

2 tablespoons extra virgin olive oil

a bunch of chives, finely chopped

sea salt and freshly ground black pepper

serves 4

Cook the pappardelle in a large saucepan of boiling, salted water until *al dente*, or according to the directions on the packet. Add the courgette slices to the pasta for the final 3 minutes of cooking.

Put the lemon zest and juice into a bowl, add the oil and mix. Add the chives, salt and pepper.

Drain the pasta and courgettes and return them to the pan. Add the lemon juice mixture and toss well to coat, then serve with the roasted salmon.

marbled chocolate cakes

The trick to these indulgent little charms is to put the chocolate chunks into the freezer before you make them, so they don't burn while the cake mix is cooking. They are best eaten 10 minutes after cooking, while the chocolate is soft and runny, but they can be left to cool and reheated for one minute on HIGH in the microwave. Take care, as the chocolate can get extremely hot when microwaved.

100 g dark chocolate (70 per cent cocoa solids), broken into 4 chunks

100 g white chocolate, broken into 4 chunks

175 g butter

175 g soft brown sugar

3 large eggs

2 tablespoons cocoa powder

175 g self-raising flour

vanilla ice cream or whipped cream, to serve

a 12-hole muffin tin

8 large paper muffin cases

serves 4

Put the chunks of chocolate into the freezer. Arrange the muffin cases in 8 of the holes in the muffin tin .

Put the butter and sugar into a bowl and, using electric beaters, beat until smooth and creamy. Add the eggs and cocoa powder and beat again until blended. Using a large metal spoon, fold in the flour, then fill the muffin cases to just over half full. Add a chunk of dark and white chocolate to each cake, pushing each one lightly into the mixture.

Cook on the middle shelf of a preheated oven at 180°C (350°F) Gas 4 for 18–20 minutes. Remove from the oven and let cool in the tray for 5–10 minutes. Peel away the muffin cases and serve warm with generous dollops of vanilla ice cream or whipped cream.

beach banquet

the scene

In my dreams, I have a beautiful house far away from any towns, surrounded by sand, sea and the odd palm tree. It's good to have dreams – they always make me smile on a rainy day. But I would share this state of bliss with friends, serving the most delicious food and wine, sitting in the sunshine, eating and laughing in this happy pleasure zone.

the style

A beautiful table on the beach set with simple china and cutlery – pure and soothing to the eye. The colour comes from the food, natural surroundings and happy people. Decorate the table with seashells, driftwood and pebbles from the beach.

summer fresh tomato toasts

These are do-it-yourself, so really couldn't be fresher. The taste relies on the garlic being very fresh and clean in its flavour, and the tomatoes being ripe, in season and packed with a true tomato flavour. This may seem a little messy, but you are eating by the sea, so a little dip could be taken between courses, or have extra napkins on the table.

12 ripe tomatoes	**TO SERVE**
8 slices bread	16 asparagus spears, cooked and cooled
8 garlic cloves, halved crossways	2 handfuls of rocket
extra virgin olive oil, for sprinkling	serves 8
sea salt and freshly ground black pepper	

Cut a cross in each tomato and put into a bowl. Cover with boiling water and leave for 30 seconds, then drain and peel. Toast the bread and let cool in a toast rack.

Arrange plates of toasted bread, garlic, small jugs or bottles of olive oil, tomatoes and sea salt and pepper. Encourage everyone to rub the toast with the garlic, sprinkle with olive oil, rub with tomato halves or top with slices of tomato, then sprinkle with salt and pepper. Serve with the asparagus spears and rocket.

THE WORK PLAN

the day before

- Make the shortbread – bake, cover and store in a cool place.
- Cook the lobsters, if using fresh ones. Remove the flesh, cover and chill.
- Cook the potatoes for the lobster salad, cover and chill.
- Peel the tomatoes for the tomato toasts, wrap and chill.

on the day

- Make the chilli dressing.
- Cook the asparagus for the tomato toasts, let cool, then cover.

just before serving

- Assemble the lobster salad.
- Toast the bread.

THE MENU
SERVES 8

Summer Fresh Tomato Toasts

Lobster Salad with Chilli Dressing

Coconut and Passionfruit Shortbread Bake

TO DRINK

Chardonnay, Riesling, Rosé, Marsala

lobster salad with chilli dressing

Ready-cooked and halved lobsters are easy to find, and some people may prefer to buy them like this rather than prepare them from scratch. But, if you have time and want to cook them yourself, it's well worth it, because you can guarantee that the lobster will be really fresh. If lobsters are difficult to get, or too expensive, try substituting monkfish, often called 'poor man's lobster', or even boneless chicken breasts, tossed in olive oil, then roasted in a hot oven for about 25 minutes. Deseed the chillies only if you are fearful of heat: I love it, so I leave them in, but it's up to you.

8 small or 4 large lobsters

650 g potatoes, cut into chunks

a bunch of coriander, coarsely chopped

1 red onion, very finely sliced

sea salt and freshly ground black pepper

leafy salad, to serve

CHILLI DRESSING

1 green or red chilli, deseeded (optional) and chopped

5 cm fresh ginger, peeled and chopped

5 garlic cloves, crushed

2 tablespoons white wine vinegar

6 tablespoons unrefined caster sugar

serves 8

To make the dressing, put the chilli, ginger and garlic into a saucepan. Add the vinegar and sugar and simmer over low heat, stirring frequently, for 10 minutes, until reduced by half. Add 2 tablespoons water, remove from the heat and let cool.

If cooking the lobsters live, bring a large saucepan of water to the boil. Plunge the lobsters carefully into the boiling water, cover with a lid and simmer for 10 minutes per 500 g. Drain and let cool.

When cool, remove the claws and legs. Using a large, sharp knife, split each body in half lengthways, holding the lobster with a tea towel in your other hand to stop it slipping. Crack open the claws and remove the flesh, leaving it in whole pieces. Remove the flesh from the split body halves and cut into thick slices. Reserve the shells.

Cook the potatoes in a saucepan of boiling, salted water for 20 minutes, until tender when pierced with a knife. Drain and let cool. Add the coriander and chopped lobster to the potatoes, with salt and pepper to taste. Mix lightly, then spoon the mixture into the empty lobster shells, piling it in generously. Spoon over the dressing, sprinkle with the onion slices and serve with a leafy salad. (If using monkfish or chicken serve from a dish decorated with lettuce leaves.)

SHORTBREAD

100 g butter

100 g unrefined caster sugar

150 g plain flour

FILLING

7 passionfruit, halved

3 eggs

75 g unrefined caster sugar

75 g desiccated coconut

60 g plain flour

150 ml coconut milk

1 tablespoon icing sugar, for dusting

Greek yoghurt and cream, or vanilla ice cream, to serve

a springform cake tin, 20 cm diameter, lightly buttered

serves 8

coconut and passionfruit shortbread bake

I love dishes that you make the day before – not only is there less to do on the day but this one actually improves from resting in a cool cupboard, so what could be better? The sweetness of the coconut is balanced by the tartness of the passionfruit, creating an elegant pudding.

To make the pastry put the butter and sugar into a bowl and beat with an electric whisk or wooden spoon until creamy. Add the flour and rub it in with your fingertips until the mixture looks like breadcrumbs. Transfer to the prepared cake tin and flatten gently with the palm of your hand and fingers, lining the base and sides of the tin. Chill while you make the filling.

Using a teaspoon, scoop the passionfruit pulp into a small bowl. Put the eggs and sugar into a large bowl and beat with an electric beater until creamy and doubled in volume. Add the desiccated coconut, flour, coconut milk and passionfruit. Using a large metal spoon, fold until evenly mixed.

Spoon the mixture into the chilled pastry case and bake in a preheated oven at 180°C (350°F) Gas 4 for 40 minutes. Remove and let cool for 10 minutes, then remove from the tin to a serving plate. Dust with icing sugar and serve with a mixture of Greek yoghurt and cream, or with ice cream.

THE MENU

FOR 8 PEOPLE

**Feta and Mushroom
Bread Tarts**

**Spicy-crust Roasted
Rack of Lamb**

**Mashed Minty Potatoes
and Peas**

Paradise Meringues

TO DRINK

**Gewürztraminer or Riesling
with the Tarts,
Cabernet Sauvignon or Shiraz
(Syrah) with the Lamb,
Sauternes with the
Meringues**

smart dining

the scene

This is formal, grown-up entertaining – for the boss, work associates, or anyone you'd like to impress. The three-course menu is modern and beautifully elegant.

the style

The perfect occasion to get out that matching tableware. For the newly married couple, there is no other time in life when those wedding presents will be as perfect as this. Decorate the table with a few simple stems and try to keep the look clean and uncluttered.

spicy-crust roasted rack of lamb

3 tablespoons cumin seeds

2 tablespoons coriander seeds

2 teaspoons black peppercorns

4 cloves

4 small dried chillies

2 tablespoons sea salt

grated zest and freshly squeezed juice of 2 unwaxed lemons

4 tablespoons olive oil

3 racks of lamb, 6 cutlets each

200 ml red wine

mashed minty potatoes and peas, to serve (see opposite)

serves 8

Heat a dry frying pan and add the cumin and coriander seeds, peppercorns, cloves and chillies. Cook for 1 minute, stirring frequently. Crush coarsely with a mortar and pestle. Transfer to a bowl and stir in the salt, lemon zest and juice and oil.

Put the racks of lamb into a large roasting tin. Rub the mixture into the lamb, smearing well all over. Cover and chill overnight.

Cook the lamb in a preheated oven at 200°C (400°F) Gas 6 for 20 minutes then reduce to 180°C (350°F) Gas 4. Cook for a further 20 minutes for rare lamb, 25 minutes for medium and 35 minutes for well done. Remove from the oven, transfer to a carving board and let rest for 5 minutes in a warm place.

Meanwhile, add the wine and 200 ml water to the roasting tin and set it on top of the stove over high heat. Stir to scrape up all the roasted bits on the bottom, and boil until reduced by half.

Cut the lamb into separate cutlets and arrange on top of the mashed minty potatoes and peas. Spoon a little sauce over the top and serve.

feta and mushroom bread tarts

This may be a formal meal, but that doesn't mean that it has to be complicated – this is a simple recipe with delicious flavours.

2 garlic cloves, crushed

4 tablespoons olive oil, plus extra for sprinkling

8 slices white crusty bread

8 portobello mushrooms, stalks removed

4 large tomatoes, quartered and deseeded

200 g feta cheese, crumbled

sea salt and freshly ground black pepper

basil or sage, chopped, to serve

serves 8

Put the garlic into a small bowl, add the olive oil and mix. Smear or brush over both sides of the bread and transfer to a roasting tin. Put a mushroom on each slice of bread. Put 2 tomato quarters on each mushroom and sprinkle with the crumbled feta.

Sprinkle with olive oil, salt and pepper, then cook in a preheated oven at 180°C (350°F) Gas 4 for 25 minutes until the bread is golden. Top with your chosen herb and serve hot or warm.

mashed minty potatoes and peas

This simple combination creates a two-in-one vegetable dish, making life in the kitchen a little easier. The mashed potato mixture can be prepared in advance, but don't add the mint until just before serving or it will lose its vibrant, fresh look.

1.5 kg boiling potatoes, cut into equal pieces

50 g butter

1 egg, beaten

100 ml milk

300 g frozen baby peas

a bunch of mint, chopped

sea salt and freshly ground black pepper

serves 8

Cook the potatoes in a large saucepan of boiling, salted water for about 20 minutes, or until tender when pierced with a knife. Drain well and return them to the pan. Shake the pan a few times, then put over low heat for 2 minutes to steam off any excess moisture.

Add the butter, egg, milk, salt and pepper. Stir briefly, then remove from the heat and crush the potatoes briefly with the back of a wooden spoon. Keep the potatoes warm while you cook the peas.

Bring a saucepan of salted water to the boil, add the peas and cook for 2 minutes. Drain, add to the potatoes, then add the mint. Mix gently, crushing the peas lightly into the potato, but keeping some whole.

THE WORK PLAN

the day before

- Make the meringues (up to a week in advance) and store in an airtight container.
- Prepare the spicy crust, rub it into the lamb, cover and chill.

on the day

- Peel the potatoes and cover with cold water.
- Make the berry cream and assemble the meringues up to 2 hours in advance. Chill.
- Brush the bread for the mushroom tarts with garlic and oil. Top with the remaining ingredients and put onto the baking sheet, ready to cook.

just before serving

- Roast the lamb.
- Cook the potatoes and peas. Put into a bowl and keep them warm.
- Remove the lamb from the oven and keep it warm.
- Cook the feta and mushroom tarts and make the sauce for the lamb.
- Carve the lamb, mix the peas and potatoes.

paradise meringues

These can be made up to a week in advance and then stored in an airtight plastic bag: use a straw to suck out all the excess air, tie up well and store in a cool, dry place.

Put both sugars into a bowl and mix. Put the egg whites into a large, clean bowl and whisk until stiff. Add half the sugar mixture and whisk again until shiny and stiff. Add the remaining sugar and whisk again briefly. Put dessertspoons of the mixture onto the prepared baking sheet, leaving space between each to allow them to spread as they cook. Cook in a preheated oven at 110°C (225°F) Gas 1/2 for 90 minutes until dry and hard. Remove and let cool.

Put the cream into a bowl and whisk until just stiff. Add half the berries and mix briefly to create a marbled effect. Sandwich the meringues together with the berry cream and transfer to individual plates or one serving plate. Sprinkle the remaining berries over the plate, cover and chill for up to 2 hours before serving.

100 g unrefined
caster sugar

100 g soft light brown
sugar

4 egg whites

300 ml double cream

500 g mixed berries,
such as raspberries,
strawberries, blueberries
or blackberries

*a baking sheet, lined with
bakewell paper*

serves 8

after the main event

the scene

If you have a big family celebration with a marquee, why not make full use of it the following day for a more relaxed, intimate party. It gives everyone the opportunity to discuss the previous day's events, and the menu is completely cook-ahead, so there isn't much to do on the day.

the style

Marquees have a summery feel, with garden furniture and soft cushions and all the flowers still looking their best. Put all the food out on a table and get everyone to help themselves – this is a family and close friends affair, so a bit of informality will be very welcome.

THE WORK PLAN

the day before

- Make the meringues up to a week in advance and store in a sealed plastic bag (use a straw to suck out all the excess air).
- Make the osso buco up to 3 days in advance, cover and chill.
- Poach the peaches and pears up to 2 days in advance, cover and chill.

on the day

- Assemble the coffee and nut meringue layer up to 2 hours in advance. Store at room temperature.

just before serving

- Put the pears into a serving dish.
- Reheat the osso buco.
- Peel and cook the potatoes.
- Prepare the beans and garlic.
- Make the gremolata, then cook the beans and mash the potatoes.

THE MENU

FOR 8 PEOPLE

Osso Buco with Gremolata

Garlic Sautéed Green Beans

Creamy Mashed Potatoes

Coffee and Nut Layer Meringue

Poached Pears and Peaches in Spiced Wine

TO DRINK

Pinot Noir with the Osso Buco, Sauternes with the Puddings

osso buco with gremolata

This dish improves when reheated – it makes a richer, silkier sauce. For the last 1½ hours of cooking, you can put this into the oven at 180°C (350°F) Gas 4 instead of on top of the stove – but make sure the casserole is flameproof. Gremolata is the traditional accompaniment for osso buco, but it is also lovely with fish, barbecues and white meat roasts. Make at the last minute, to preserve its herby zing.

OSSO BUCO

8 shins of veal with the marrow bone, 300 g each

4 tablespoons plain flour

4 tablespoons olive oil

3 garlic cloves, crushed and chopped

2 onions, chopped

4 celery stalks, chopped

1 tablespoon tomato purée

2 cans chopped tomatoes, 410 g each

200 ml dry white wine

300 ml vegetable stock

sea salt and freshly ground black pepper

GREMOLATA

finely grated zest of 3 unwaxed lemons

3 garlic cloves, finely chopped

a large bunch of fresh flat leaf parsley, finely chopped

serves 8

Dust the veal shins with flour. Heat the oil in a large saucepan, add the veal and fry over medium-low heat for a few minutes, until brown all over. Remove from the pan and set aside.

Add a little more oil to the pan if needed, heat and add the garlic, onions and celery. Cook for 5 minutes until soft but not browned. Add the tomato purée and tomatoes, mix well and add the wine, stock and salt and pepper to taste. Return the meat to the pan and gently bring to the boil. Cover with a lid and simmer gently for 1½ hours, adding a little more stock or wine from time to time if needed. Let cool, cover and chill.

When ready to serve, put the osso buco into a preheated oven at 180°C (350°F) Gas 4 until simmering, then continue cooking for 15 minutes or until heated right through.

Meanwhile, to make the gremolata, put the lemon zest, garlic and parsley into a bowl and stir well.

Remove the osso buco from the oven and serve topped with gremolata.

garlic sautéed green beans

It may seem odd not to cook the beans in a pan of water, but with this method the beans take on a wonderful buttery, garlic flavour, while keeping their crunchy texture.

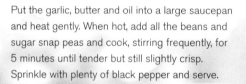

2 garlic cloves, crushed and finely chopped	200 g fine green beans, trimmed
25 g butter	200 g sugar snap peas, trimmed
2 tablespoons olive oil	freshly ground black pepper
200 g flat beans, trimmed and cut into 3 pieces each	serves 8

Put the garlic, butter and oil into a large saucepan and heat gently. When hot, add all the beans and sugar snap peas and cook, stirring frequently, for 5 minutes until tender but still slightly crisp. Sprinkle with plenty of black pepper and serve.

creamy mashed potatoes

All sorts of different and wonderful flavours can be added to mashed potatoes. However, since the osso buco has such richly intense flavour, this time keep the potatoes plain. If serving with simpler flavours, such as grilled fish or lamb chops, try adding chopped herbs, cheese such as goats', blue or mascarpone, saffron threads (just steep in a little hot water before adding), wholegrain mustard or spring onions.

1.5 kg potatoes, cut into equal pieces

50 g butter

4 tablespoons olive oil

100 ml cream or milk

2 heaped teaspoons English mustard powder, mixed to a paste with water

sea salt and freshly ground black pepper

serves 8

Cook the potatoes in a saucepan of boiling, salted water for 20 minutes, until tender when pierced with a knife. Drain well and return to the pan. Set over low heat for 2 minutes to steam off the excess moisture. Remove from the heat and mash thoroughly. Add the butter, oil, cream or milk, mustard and salt and pepper to taste. Mix well, or blend until smooth and creamy with an electric beater.

coffee and nut layer meringue

To be sure of even cooking, you may need to switch the meringues from shelf to shelf at various stages during cooking.

6 egg whites

375 g unrefined caster sugar

100 g chopped mixed nuts

600 ml double cream

2 tablespoons icing sugar, plus extra for dusting

1 tablespoon instant coffee

100 g chopped walnuts

3 baking sheets, lined with bakewell paper

serves 8

Put a dinner plate upside down on each lined baking sheet and draw around it with a dark-coloured pen. Turn the paper over and use the circles as your guideline.

Put the egg whites into a large, clean bowl and whisk until stiff and fluffy. Add half the sugar and whisk again until smooth and shiny. Add the remaining sugar and nuts and whisk briefly. Divide the mixture between the 3 drawn circles on the baking sheets. Spread out with the back of a spoon to fill the circles. Bake in a preheated oven at 140°C (275°F) Gas 1 for 1 hour, until firm on the outside but still soft in the middle.

Put the cream into a bowl and whisk until soft. Put the icing sugar and coffee into a cup and add just enough boiling water to dissolve the coffee. Add the coffee and walnuts to the cream and mix carefully until evenly blended.

To assemble, put a spoonful of cream onto a large serving plate: this will help secure the meringue. Put one of the meringue layers on top and spread with half the cream mixture. Add another meringue layer and spread with the remaining cream mixture. Top with the final meringue layer and dust with icing sugar. Chill for up to 2 hours before serving.

poached pears and peaches in spiced wine

These can be served on their own or with the coffee and nut layer meringue. Buy ripe and juicy peaches – the stones are easier to remove.

8 pears, peeled with stalk still attached

1 bottle red wine, 750 ml

1 star anise

2 cardamom pods

4 cloves

1 unwaxed lemon, sliced

100 g unrefined caster sugar

4 peaches, halved crossways and pitted

serves 8

Put the pears into a saucepan and add the wine, star anise, cardamom pods, cloves, lemon slices and sugar. Slowly bring to the boil, then simmer for 15 minutes. Remove from the heat and add the peach halves. Set aside for 1 hour to infuse. Serve warm or cold with the coffee and nut layer meringue, or with cream or mascarpone.

THE WORK PLAN

the day before

- Marinate the chicken, cover and chill.
- Roast the rice for the duck salad. Roast the duck, make the dressing, cover and chill.

on the day

- Make the syrup banana rice cake. (Reheat in the pan briefly before turning it out onto a plate, to stop it sticking.)
- Cook the chicken.
- Make the laksa, but don't add the spring onions.

just before serving

- Assemble the duck salad.
- Make the fruit salad.

THE MENU
FOR 8 PEOPLE

Seafood Laksa

Thai-style Duck Salad

Korean Chicken

Exotic Fruit Salad

Syrup Banana Rice Cake

TO DRINK

Lager, Riesling, Pinot Noir

the scene

This sort of feast is a real treat for the taste buds, and with all the ingredients readily available, you can recreate that Asian restaurant in your own home.

the style

Let your imagination run wild and indulge in all those exotic, dramatic eastern looks – a low table, a colourful runner down the middle, chopsticks and exotic flowers.

eastern feast

seafood laksa

This is a meal in itself and always hugely popular.

200 g rice noodles

2 tablespoons peanut oil

1 onion, sliced

2 garlic cloves, crushed and chopped

5 cm fresh ginger, peeled and chopped

1 stalk of lemongrass, bruised and chopped

1 red chilli, finely sliced

600 g uncooked, peeled tiger prawns

1/2 teaspoon ground turmeric

1/2 teaspoon ground coriander

500 ml coconut milk

800 ml fish or vegetable stock

1 tablespoon fish sauce

freshly squeezed juice of 1 lime

200 g fresh beansprouts

a bunch of spring onions, sliced

serves 8

Put the noodles into a bowl and cover with boiling water. Let soak until soft, about 10 minutes, or according to the directions on the packet, then drain.

Heat the oil in a large saucepan and add the onion, garlic, ginger, lemongrass, chilli and prawns. Cook over medium heat for 5 minutes, stirring frequently. Add the turmeric and coriander and cook for a further 2 minutes. Add the coconut milk, stock, fish sauce, lime juice, beansprouts, noodles and spring onions. Mix well and bring to a very gentle simmer for about 2 minutes, then serve.

Thai-style duck salad

This duck salad may seem a bit long and complicated, but every time I serve it, everyone has been fascinated and wants to know how I made it. So, if you have inquisitive taste buds, I urge you to try this dish. Prawns, beef or pork can be used instead of the duck.

75 g fragrant Thai rice

4 duck legs

1 tablespoon fish sauce

5 cm fresh ginger, peeled and chopped

5 cm galangal or extra fresh ginger, peeled and chopped

3 stalks of lemongrass, finely sliced

6 kaffir lime leaves

100 ml coconut milk

3 green mangoes, peeled and cut into matchsticks

100 g Chinese yard-long beans, finely sliced

2 chillies, finely chopped

100 g Chinese cabbage or iceberg lettuce, shredded

a bunch of Thai basil

a bunch of coriander, chopped

50 g cashew nuts, chopped, to serve

DRESSING

1 bird's eye chilli, deseeded and chopped

1 tablespoon fish sauce

freshly squeezed juice of 3 limes

1 teaspoon tamarind paste

serves 8

Put the rice into a bowl, cover with cold water and soak for 5 minutes. Drain, then sprinkle evenly over a baking sheet. Cook in a preheated oven at 200°C (400°F) Gas 6 for 30 minutes until golden and starting to pop. Crush coarsely with a mortar and pestle. Keep the oven at the same temperature.

Put the duck legs into a roasting tin and add the fish sauce, ginger, galangal, if using, lemongrass, 4 of the lime leaves and the coconut milk. Transfer to the preheated oven and cook for 30 minutes, then reduce to 180°C (350°F) Gas 4 and cook for a further 40 minutes, until the skin is golden and crisp. Remove from the oven and let cool. When cool, shred the duck into bite-sized pieces, discarding the bones, and put into a large bowl with all the bits and juices from the roasting tin.

Add the mango, yard-long beans, chillies and cabbage or lettuce to the bowl. Finely shred the remaining 2 lime leaves and add to the bowl. Just before serving add the basil leaves, coriander and crushed rice and mix well.

To make the dressing, put the chilli, fish sauce, lime juice and tamarind paste into a small bowl or jug. Stir well, then just before serving, pour over the salad and toss gently. Sprinkle with chopped cashews and serve.

korean chicken

Remove any excess fat from the chicken pieces and drain off the oil while cooking.

2 kg chicken pieces, trimmed

4 tablespoons sesame oil

100 ml light soy sauce

4 garlic cloves, crushed and very finely chopped

1 teaspoon chilli powder

5 spring onions, very finely chopped

freshly ground black pepper

TO SERVE

500 g dried egg noodles

1 teaspoon black sesame seeds (optional)

serves 8

Put the chicken into an ovenproof dish, add the sesame oil, soy sauce, garlic, chilli powder, spring onions and black pepper to taste. Mix well, cover and chill overnight.

Uncover the chicken and cook in a preheated oven at 180°C (350°F) Gas 4 for 30 minutes. Reduce to 140°C (275°F) Gas 1 and cook for a further 40 minutes. Meanwhile, cook the noodles according to the directions on the packet. Drain, then serve the chicken and noodles, sprinkled with the black sesame seeds, if using.

exotic fruit salad

Not an apple or orange in sight in this exotic fruit salad. I like it to be full of fruit from the tropics, chosen according to cost and what's in season. Include no more than four varieties, so the individual flavours will be strong and sharp.

choose from sweet pineapple, mango, papaya, bananas, lychee, fresh coconut, watermelon, melon, pomegranate, passionfruit or persimmon

freshly squeezed juice of 4 limes

serves 8

Prepare the chosen fruits, arrange on a serving dish, then squeeze the juice of 4 limes over the top.

syrup banana rice cake

If South-east Asia were to have a version of tarte Tatin, this would be it – if you like sticky hot bananas and rice pudding, this was invented for you.

75 g brown sugar

25 g butter

6 bananas, sliced

175 g white rice, cooked, drained and cooled

2 eggs, beaten

1/2 teaspoon vanilla extract

1/2 teaspoon freshly grated nutmeg

50 g unrefined caster sugar

100 g self-raising flour

serves 8

Put the brown sugar and butter into an ovenproof frying pan and put over medium-high heat. When melted and bubbling, add the bananas, in layers. Put the cooked rice, egg, vanilla extract and nutmeg into a bowl and mix. Add the caster sugar and flour and stir until smooth. Spoon the mixture over the bananas, spreading it evenly with the back of a spoon. Transfer the pan to a preheated oven and bake at 180°C (350°F) Gas 4 for 35 minutes until set and golden. Let cool for 5 minutes, then turn out, banana side up, onto a large plate. Serve warm, at room temperature or cold.

teenage party

the scene

Friends are of the utmost importance when you are a teenager. Parties are an essential part of this exciting stage of life: the music, the clothes, the dancing – and of course the food as well.

the style

Set out the food and accessories on a table, for people to help themselves. Have lots of napkins, straws, glasses and extra plates – the food is so good they will keep coming back for more.

THE MENU

FOR 24 PEOPLE

Chicken Sticks
with Sweet
Chilli

Herby
Hamburgers

Potato Skins
with Green Dip

Vegetarian
Mexican Rolls

Chocolate Chip
Cookie Ice
Cream Cakes

DRINKS

Apple and Mint
Fizz,
Ginger Beer

apple and mint fizz

There is something satisfying and traditional about making your own drinks. This one is simple, refreshing and also popular on hot summer days.

a large bunch of
mint

2 litres apple juice

1 litre sparkling
mineral water

ice cubes, to serve

makes about
3.5 litres

Reserve some of the mint leaves for serving and put the remainder into a heat-proof jug. Add 300 ml boiling water, et cool, then chill.

Transfer to a large container and add the apple juice, mineral water and ice cubes. Chop the reserved mint leaves, sprinkle over the top and serve.

ginger beer

This seems a large quantity of ginger beer but it's so easy to make and it does store well. Take care that the bottle tops are secure, as they can sometimes pop off.

3 unwaxed lemons

625 g unrefined
caster sugar

200 g fresh ginger,
peeled and sliced

5 g cream of tartar

1 tablespoon brewer's
yeast

makes about 6 litres

Cut the yellow zest off the lemons in strips, then remove and discard the white pith. Finely slice the lemon flesh, removing all the pips. Put the lemon flesh and zest into a large bowl and add the sugar, ginger and cream of tartar. Add about 6 litres boiling water and let stand until tepid.

Sprinkle in the yeast and stir. Cover with clingfilm and let stand in a warm place for 24 hours. Using a large metal spoon, skim off the yeast, then carefully strain the mixture through a sieve, leaving behind any sediment. Pour into bottles with secure tops and leave for 2 days before drinking. Serve chilled with ice.

chicken sticks with sweet chilli

Chicken sticks are always very popular, so it's worth making extra. You can use boneless chicken thighs, but always remove any excess fat. They may also need to cook for a little longer, as the meat is denser.

12 boneless, skinless chicken breasts, cut into 10 cubes each

400 ml sweet chilli sauce

olive oil, for brushing

24 bamboo satay sticks, soaked in water for about 30 minutes

serves 24

Put the chicken and sweet chilli sauce into a bowl and mix well. Cover and chill overnight. When ready to cook, thread the chicken cubes onto the soaked satay sticks. Heat the grill to medium-high and brush the rack of the grill pan with oil.

Add the chicken sticks to the rack and cook, in batches if necessary, turning frequently, for 25 minutes, or until the chicken is cooked through. Repeat until all the chicken sticks are cooked, then serve hot or cold.

herby hamburgers

The best way to get a good, even mixture is with your hands. Don't be tempted to use those synthetic burger buns – a good, crusty roll makes all the difference.

1.25 kg best quality beef mince

8 shallots, finely chopped

5 garlic cloves, chopped

a bunch of flat leaf parsley, chopped

a bunch of chives, chopped

a bunch of tarragon, chopped

2 teaspoons sea salt

2 teaspoons freshly ground black pepper

3 tablespoons Worcestershire sauce

1 teaspoon Tabasco sauce

TO SERVE

crusty rolls or ciabatta rolls

beef tomatoes, sliced

rocket or watercress

red onions, finely sliced

spring onions

mustard, mayonnaise, tomato ketchup

greaseproof paper

serves 24

Put all the burger ingredients into a large bowl and, using your hands, mix for about 5 minutes until evenly blended. Divide the mixture into 24, roll into balls and pat into hamburger shapes. Arrange in layers on a large plate with squares of greaseproof paper between each burger. Cover and chill until needed.

Cook at a high heat either on a preheated barbecue or in a frying pan, preferably non-stick, for 3 minutes on each side for medium and 5 minutes each side for well done.

Set out all the burger ingredients and let people assemble their own.

potato skins with green dip

You can have the cheese either melted and soft or crisp and crunchy – check as they cook and remove at the right moment. Save the potato middles for another day.

12 large baking potatoes

200 ml olive oil

400 g mature Cheddar cheese, grated

GREEN DIP

400 ml sour cream

2 bunches of chives, chopped

2 bunches of spring onions, chopped

a bunch of flat leaf parsley, chopped

sea salt and freshly ground black pepper

a baking sheet, lightly oiled

serves 24

Using a small, sharp knife, pierce each potato right through the middle. Bake in a preheated oven at 180°C (350°F) Gas 4 for 1 hour 10 minutes until cooked through. Remove and set aside until cool enough to handle. Cut each potato in half lengthways and, using a dessertspoon, scoop out the soft potato middles, leaving a thin layer lining the skin. Cut each skin half into 4 wedges, then cover and chill until needed.

Brush oil over the potato skins and arrange in a single layer on the prepared baking sheet. Bake at the top of a preheated oven at 220°C (425°F) Gas 7 for 30 minutes until golden, moving the potatoes around occasionally to ensure even cooking. Remove from the oven and reduce the heat to 200°C (400°F) Gas 6. Sprinkle with cheese and return to the oven for 5–10 minutes, until the cheese is melted or crunchy, checking after 5 minutes if you want it melted.

To make the dip, put the sour cream, chives, spring onions and parsley into a bowl. Add salt and pepper to taste and mix well. Serve with the potato skins for dipping.

vegetarian mexican rolls

These are best made to order or at the last moment, otherwise the avocado will discolour. You could encourage everyone to roll their own by setting out all the fillings in bowls and leaving the avocados whole, for everyone to slice as needed.

12 soft large flour tortillas

200 g cream cheese

4 carrots, grated

a bunch of coriander, chopped

a bunch of chives, chopped

a bunch of spring onions, chopped

2 chillies, chopped

4 avocados, halved, pitted, peeled and sliced

freshly squeezed juice of 2 lemons

4 tablespoons olive oil, plus extra to serve

sea salt and freshly ground black pepper

serves 24

Cook the tortillas according to the directions on the packet. Let cool, then put each tortilla on an individual sheet of clingfilm. Spread with the cream cheese and then sprinkle evenly with the carrot, coriander, chives, spring onions and chillies. Flatten the topping lightly with a palette knife.

Put the avocado slices into a bowl and sprinkle with lemon juice, oil, salt and pepper. Arrange over the open tortillas. Roll each tortilla into a tight cylinder, using the clingfilm to help you roll. Twist both ends in opposite directions to make a cigar shape. Chill until needed, then slice in half, with the clingfilm still on, and serve.

375 g butter

375 g unrefined
caster sugar

3 eggs

1 teaspoon vanilla
extract

375 g plain flour

375 g dark
chocolate (70 per
cent cocoa solids),
chopped

2.5 litres ice cream

*2 baking sheets,
lined with
bakewell paper*

serves 24

chocolate chip cookie
ice cream cakes

What a combination! Two of my
favourite sweet things sandwiched
together. If you really do run out of
time and can't make the cookies
then by all means buy them, but they
will not be as good as my recipe!

Put the butter and sugar into a bowl and beat until light and fluffy.
Add the eggs and vanilla and beat well. (The mixture will separate,
but this is not a problem.) Add the flour and chocolate and fold until
smooth. Working in batches, spoon out 48 portions of the mixture
(2 teaspoons each) onto the prepared baking sheets, making sure
each biscuit has enough room to spread (they will triple in size).
Bake in the middle of a preheated oven at 180°C (350°F) Gas 4
for about 15 minutes until lightly golden. Remove from the oven
and let cool on the baking sheets for 5 minutes. Transfer to a wire
cooling rack and let cool completely.

Sandwich 2 biscuits together with ice cream, arrange on a tray,
cover well with foil and return to the freezer until needed. Remove
20 minutes before serving so the ice cream can soften a little.

waterside
feast

the scene

If I had a house by the
sea or a river, I would
have a party like this
once a week. Just
imagine swimming,
eating, chatting, eating,
dipping, laughing and
eating again – it's such
an easy, happy way to
socialize, and the
variety of dishes
breaks up the formality
of a three-course meal.
It's the sort of
gathering that might
start at midday and roll
on until dusk. The trick
with the food is to
avoid putting it all out
at once and to
encourage guests to
cook their own.

the style

A little organization is
needed with this
gathering, but it is very
flexible. You really don't
want to be scraping
plates and washing up
– so go on, be brave
and pay someone to
come and do it for you.
Set a really large table
with all the abundance
of the feast and have
the barbecue nearby.
Use a separate table
for drinks and chill
your bottles in groovy-
coloured plastic boxes.

THE MENU

FOR 20 PEOPLE

Vodka Watermelon

**Sesame-crusted
Marlin with Ginger
Dressing**

**Pork Satay
with Spiced Dip**

**Sweet Glazed
Pepper Salad**

**Mozzarella Baked
Tomatoes**

Noodle Mountain

**Blue and Red Berry
Tarts**

TO DRINK

**Pinot Blanc,
Chardonnay**

THE WORK PLAN

the day before

- Make the tart cases, store in a cool place.
- Prepare the pork and marinate overnight.
- Prepare the tomatoes, cover and chill.

on the day

- Make the vodka watermelon and chill.
- Cook the peppers and onions.
- Dip the marlin steaks in sesame seeds,
  cover and chill until needed.
- Make the ginger dressing.
- Make the spiced dip for the pork.

just before serving

- Assemble the fruit tarts.
- Cook the marlin, pork and tomatoes.
- Assemble the pepper salad.
- Make the noodle mountain.

vodka watermelon

This tastes and looks heavenly, but has the effect of dynamite! If you can't get seedless watermelon, just use regular and deseed it.

1 seedless watermelon, chilled

1 bottle chilled vodka, 750 ml

lime wedges and ice, to serve

serves 20

Cut the melon in half and scoop out all the flesh. Put into a blender and process until smooth. Remove to a large jug, add the vodka and let chill for 2 hours before serving. For a less alcoholic version, add sparkling mineral water, or lemonade for those with a sweet tooth. Serve with lime wedges and ice.

sesame-crusted marlin with ginger dressing

Marlin is fantastic for the barbecue, as it is firm and doesn't break up when turned. It's a dense fish with an intense flavour, so serve it in small portions. Swordfish also works well.

20 marlin or swordfish steaks, 100 g each

5 egg whites*

750 g toasted sesame seeds

1 tablespoon crushed dried chillies

GINGER DRESSING

400 g fresh ginger, peeled and finely chopped

600 ml light soy sauce

2 bunches of spring onions, chopped

4 tablespoons sesame oil

serves 20

Dry the marlin steaks with kitchen paper. Put the egg whites into a bowl and whisk until frothy. Put the sesame seeds and dried chillies onto a large plate and mix. Dip each marlin steak first into the egg whites, then into the sesame seeds and dried chillies, until evenly coated on both sides. Cook under a medium grill or on a preheated barbecue for 5 minutes on each side.

To make the dressing, put the ginger, soy sauce, spring onions and sesame oil into a bowl and mix. Spoon the dressing over the marlin and serve.

*Note Use the leftover egg whites from the tart pastry.

pork satay with spiced dip

This yoghurt dip is fresh and different and, as it's nut-free, it's great if you have any allergy worries. You can also use chicken or beef instead of pork.

4 pork fillets, about 400 g each, cut into 4 cm cubes

4 tablespoons mild curry powder

4 tablespoons ground coriander

375 g fresh ginger, peeled and grated

4 garlic cloves, crushed and finely chopped

4 tablespoons soy sauce

4 tablespoons vegetable oil

SPICED DIP

4 tablespoons mild curry powder

2 large bunches of coriander, chopped

500 ml Greek yoghurt

20 long metal skewers

serves 20

Put the pork into a bowl and add the curry powder, ground coriander, ginger, garlic, soy sauce, oil and 6 tablespoons water. Mix well, cover and chill for at least 1 hour, preferably overnight.

Thread the pork onto the skewers and cook under a hot grill or on a preheated barbecue for about 20 minutes, turning frequently, until cooked through.

Put the dip ingredients into a bowl and mix. Serve with the pork.

sweet glazed pepper salad

For centuries, Italians have been eating roasted peppers and they are truly wonderful. Don't think that there are far too many in this recipe. Not true – I can promise you, it will all disappear!

10 red peppers, cut into large chunks and deseeded

5 red onions, quartered lengthways

4 tablespoons olive oil

5 tablespoons balsamic vinegar

2 tablespoons runny honey

400 g pitted kalamata or other black olives, chopped

sea salt and freshly ground black pepper

a sprig of parsley, to serve

serves 20

Put the peppers and onions into a large bowl, add the olive oil and mix to coat. Transfer to 2 large roasting tins and cook in a preheated oven at 180°C (350°F) Gas 4 for 1 hour, turning the vegetables after 40 minutes so they will cook evenly. Add the vinegar, honey, olives, salt and pepper, mix well and set aside to cool. Serve warm or cold, topped with a sprig of parsley.

mozzarella baked tomatoes

If you can find it, use purple basil, which looks even more spectacular than green. This dish really couldn't be easier, and makes a nice change from roasted tomato halves.

20 ripe tomatoes

250 g mozzarella cheese, drained and cut into 20 pieces

100 ml olive oil

a bunch of basil, torn

sea salt and freshly ground black pepper

a large baking sheet, lightly oiled

serves 20

Cut a deep cross, to about half way down, in the top of each tomato and stuff a piece of mozzarella into each. Transfer to the baking sheet and sprinkle with salt and pepper. Cook in a preheated oven at 160°C (325°F) Gas 3 for 25 minutes until the tomatoes are beginning to soften and open up. Sprinkle with oil and basil and serve warm.

I love showing off in the kitchen, so cooking for friends is always great fun. Often I start to organize a small dinner and it ends up with twenty people – I just can't stop gathering everyone together!

noodle mountain

Any vegetarians at your party will be grateful for the wide selection of dishes you have provided, so don't be daunted by this large mountain – they'll love it. Other vegetables can always be added, such as asparagus, baby corn, thin green beans, carrots, mushrooms or water chestnuts.

300 g dried egg noodles

6 tablespoons vegetable oil

4 garlic cloves, crushed and chopped

12 cm fresh ginger, peeled and chopped

4 onions, finely sliced

4 chillies, finely chopped

1 Chinese cabbage, finely shredded

250 g beansprouts

200 ml soy sauce

freshly squeezed juice of 4 limes

2 bunches of spring onions, chopped

400 g cashew nuts, chopped

serves 20

Cook the noodles according to the directions on the packet, drain and transfer to a bowl of cold water until needed.

Heat the oil in a wok and add the garlic, ginger, onions and chillies. Cook over medium heat for 5 minutes until softened. Add the cabbage and beansprouts and stir briefly. Drain the noodles well and add to the wok. Toss with 2 large spoons, then add the soy sauce, lime juice, spring onions and cashew nuts. Mix well and serve.

PASTRY

750 g plain flour

150 g unrefined caster sugar

525 g butter

6 egg yolks

FILLING

300 g blueberries

250 g icing sugar, plus extra for dusting

1.2 litres double cream

1 kg strawberries, hulled and cut into bite-sized pieces

500 g raspberries

300 g blackberries

3 loose-based tart tins, 23 cm diameter, buttered

greaseproof paper and baking beans or uncooked rice

serves 20

blue and red berry tarts

Make these mixed fruit tarts and I promise you they will just disappear – no one can resist perfect crumbling pastry piled with mixed fruits and served with softly whipped cream. With this quantity of pastry, it's easiest to make it in two batches, saving the leftover egg whites for the marlin coating (page 127).

Put half the flour, half the sugar and half the butter into a food processor and blend until the mixture looks like breadcrumbs. Add 3 of the egg yolks and process again until the mixture forms a ball. Remove and repeat with the remaining pastry ingredients. Combine, then divide into 3 equal amounts. Wrap separately in clingfilm and chill for about 20 minutes.

Transfer to a lightly floured surface and roll out each pastry portion until just larger than the tart tins. Line each tin with pastry, prick the base with a fork and chill for 20 minutes.

Line the chilled pastry cases with greaseproof paper and baking beans or rice. Cook in a preheated oven at 180°C

(350°F) Gas 4 for 20 minutes. Remove the baking beans and paper, reduce to 160°C (325°F) Gas 3 and cook for a further 20 minutes until dry and golden.

Put the blueberries and half the icing sugar into a small saucepan. Add 100 ml water and simmer gently for 5 minutes until the berries are soft. Remove from the heat and let cool.

Put the cream into a bowl, add the remaining icing sugar and whisk until soft peaks form. Add the strawberries, mix briefly, then spoon into the cooled pastry cases. Pile the raspberries and blackberries on top. Spoon over the stewed blueberries, remove the tarts from the tins and serve dusted with icing sugar.

THE MENU

FOR 12 PEOPLE

Chicken Jalfrezi

Chickpea and Vegetable Curry

Crusted Rice Cake

Tomato and Onion Salad

Naan Bread and Pappadams

Caramelized Orange and Pineapple

TO DRINK

Lager, Sauvignon Blanc, Viognier

party buffet

the scene

The menu is predominantly Indian. It's great for serving to a crowd – the dishes can be made in advance and flavours will only improve.

the style

Let the interior designer in you show off with lengths of sari fabric, strings of flowers and dazzling, colourful cloth. If it's an outdoor party, put rugs on the ground and scatter cushions around a low table, for a touch of exotic decadence.

THE WORK PLAN

the day before

- Make the chicken jalfrezi, let cool, cover and chill. (Reheat gently in the oven and add lemon and herbs just before serving.)

on the day

- Soak and prepare the crusted rice cake.
- Slice the oranges and pineapple.
- Make the chickpea and vegetable curry.

just before serving

- Make the tomato and onion salad.
- Make the caramel – if you are making spun sugar, this must be done at the last minute, but if serving as a sauce, it can be made earlier in the day.

4 tablespoons
vegetable oil

3 large onions,
sliced

3 garlic cloves,
chopped

5 cm fresh ginger,
peeled and
chopped

4 chillies, chopped

2 teaspoons
ground turmeric

4 cardamom pods,
lightly crushed

4 teaspoons curry
powder

2 teaspoons
ground coriander

2 teaspoons
ground cumin

2 kg boneless,
skinless chicken
(about 2 medium
chickens), cut
into chunks

3 cans chopped
tomatoes, about
410 g each

freshly squeezed
juice of 2 limes

freshly squeezed
juice of 1 lemon

a large bunch
of coriander,
chopped, to serve

sea salt and
freshly ground
black pepper

serves 12

chicken jalfrezi

This curry can also be made with beef,
lamb, prawns or fish instead of
chicken. If using fish, choose a firm
white variety such as swordfish, marlin,
monkfish or kingfish, or whatever your
fishmonger recommends.

Heat the oil in a large saucepan, add the
onion, garlic, and chillies and cook until
soft, making sure they do not brown or
frizzle. Add the turmeric, cardamom, curry
powder, ground coriander and cumin and
cook for 2 minutes. Add the chicken, sprinkle
with salt and pepper and stir until coated
with the spices. Cook for 5 minutes until
the chicken is opaque on the outside.
Add the tomatoes, mix well, cover with a lid
and simmer for 30 minutes, stirring from
time to time. If making in advance, make
up to this point, cool and chill. Add the lime
and lemon juices, simmer for 3 minutes
and serve with the chopped coriander.

chickpea and vegetable curry

We eat a lot of this curry at home as it's simple to make and usually we have the ingredients to hand. I often call it my end-of-the-week curry when there is not much else in the house. You can change any of the vegetables to suit availability, but I always avoid carrots and peas – they don't seem authentic. As with all curries this can be made in advance and left overnight for the flavours to deepen and intensify.

3 tablespoons vegetable oil

2 garlic cloves, crushed

2 red onions, chopped

4 cm fresh ginger, peeled and diced

1 tablespoon curry powder

2 teaspoons ground coriander

1/2 teaspoon fenugreek

1/2 teaspoon crushed dried chillies

1 can chopped tomatoes, 410 g

800 g potatoes, cut into 2.5 cm pieces

1 cauliflower, cut into florets

2 cans chickpeas, 410 g each, drained and rinsed

500 g spinach, washed, dried and coarsely chopped

250 g okra, washed, dried and halved lengthways

serves 12

Heat the oil in a large saucepan, add the garlic, onion and ginger and cook over low heat for 10 minutes until softened. Add the curry powder, coriander, fenugreek and dried chillies, mix well and cook for a further 4 minutes. Add the tomatoes and 100 ml water, then add the potatoes, cauliflower and chickpeas. Mix well and simmer for 15 minutes, stirring frequently. Add the spinach and okra, mix well and simmer for 5 minutes. You may need to add a little extra water at this final stage. Serve with the chicken jalfrezi, crusted rice cake, tomato and onion salad, naan bread and pappadams.

crusted rice cake

Rice can be a delicious staple at large gatherings, and this great Persian recipe not only tastes divine but is stunning too. The trick to this dish is to use a good pan with a tight fitting lid, such as Le Creuset. A heavy frying pan will also work.

500 g basmati rice

1/2 teaspoon saffron threads

100 g butter

1 cinnamon stick

3 cloves

3 cardamom pods

50 g raisins

6 dried apricots, soaked in water for 30 minutes, then chopped

serves 12

Soak the rice in cold water for 1 hour, drain and rinse under the tap until the water runs clear. Bring a large saucepan of water to the boil, then add the rice. Simmer for 3 minutes, adding the saffron threads after 2 minutes, then drain well.

Melt 60 g of the butter in a frying pan, then add half the drained rice and flatten slightly with the back of a spoon. Remove from the heat. Put the cinnamon stick, cloves, cardamom, raisins and apricots into a bowl and mix. Spread in a layer on top of the rice. Top with the remaining rice and flatten with the back of a spoon. Cut the remaining butter into small pieces and dot over the rice. Cover the pan with a clean, dry tea towel and then with a fitted lid. Turn up and secure any excess tea towel (or tie the corners together), to stop it catching fire, and put over the lowest heat for about 30 minutes. Remove from the heat and let stand for 15 minutes with the lid on, then turn out the rice cake onto a large plate. Serve hot, at room temperature or cold.

tomato and onion salad

Be generous with parsley and coriander – they act as palate fresheners after a spicy curry.

6 beef tomatoes

2 red onions, finely sliced

1 white onion, chopped

a bunch of spring onions, sliced

a bunch of flat leaf parsley, chopped

a bunch of coriander, chopped

4 tablespoons olive oil

1 tablespoon white wine vinegar

1 tablespoon crushed mustard seeds

sea salt and freshly ground black pepper

serves 12

Cut a cross in the top of each tomato and put them into a large bowl. Cover with boiling water, leave for 30 seconds, then drain and peel. Chop the tomatoes coarsely and put into a large bowl. Add all the onion and spring onions, then add the parsley, coriander, oil, vinegar, mustard seeds, salt and pepper. Mix well and serve at room temperature.

caramelized orange and pineapple

8 large, juicy
oranges

2 sweet
pineapples

300 g unrefined
caster sugar

serves 12

If you can find really sweet pineapples, you won't need to remove the core.

Using a small, sharp knife, cut away the skin and pith from the oranges, leaving just the flesh. Cut the oranges in half lengthways, then crossways into slices.

Using a serrated knife, cut off the pineapple skin in strips, working from the top down and making sure all the little prickly black spots are removed from the flesh. Cut the pineapples into wedges lengthways and remove the cores. If the pineapple is large, cut it into chunks. Arrange the orange and pineapple on a serving dish.

Put the sugar into a saucepan, heat gently until melted and bubbling, then cook until golden brown. Remove from the heat and add 4 tablespoons water – take care, because the mixture will spatter. Stir until smooth, let cool for 5 minutes and then pour over the prepared fruit.

Note If you want to make a stunning centrepiece, try your hand at sugar-pulling. Leave a little of the sauce in the pan and, using a fork, dip into the sauce and then pull away, making long strands of sugar. Pile these on top of the fruit like a golden cobweb. The trick to sugar-pulling is the temperature of the sugar – if it runs off the fork it is too hot, so let it cool. If it is brittle and just snaps when pulled, it is too cool, so heat it carefully over a very low heat, until it is flexible. Take care not to overheat the sugar or it will burn.

drinks and fingerfood

ricepaper parcels with dipping soy

These are time-consuming but worth it, so enlist some help when assembling just before the party. Keep them chilled, covered with a damp cloth and clingfilm, until needed.

12 ricepaper wrappers*	1 tablespoon toasted sesame seeds
2 carrots, cut into matchsticks	
6 spring onions, cut into matchsticks	**DIPPING SOY**
75 g beansprouts	2 tablespoons honey
leaves from a bunch of Thai basil	1 tablespoon soy sauce
a bunch of watercress	1 tablespoon teriyaki sauce
	1 red chilli, finely sliced

serves 12

Soak the ricepaper wrappers in several changes of warm water until soft, about 4 minutes.

Gather up little clusters of the carrots, spring onions, beansprouts, basil and watercress and put in the middle of the softened wrappers. Sprinkle with sesame seeds and roll up to enclose the vegetables.

To make the dipping soy, put the honey, soy sauce and teriyaki sauce into a small bowl and mix. Add the chilli and transfer to a small, shallow dish to serve with the parcels.

*Note Thai or Vietnamese dried ricepaper wrappers (*bánh tráng*) are sold in Asian markets. Sold in packages of 50–100, they keep well in a cool cupboard.

THE MENU
FOR 12 PEOPLE

Ricepaper Parcels with Dipping Soy

Smoked Oyster and Goats' Cheese Pastries

Grissini Sticks with Parma Ham

Parmesan and Rosemary Wafers

Artichoke and Tomato Bread Puffs

Raw Vegetable Platter

TO DRINK

Cocktails (page 142)

---

the scene

It's never worth having a drinks party for fewer than 12, and they are even better with more. It's a great way to see all your friends, but it is important to serve good drinks and delicious food. I can't bear it when you go to a party and are served supermarket food and sad drinks in plastic glasses. If you don't have enough glasses, hire them from a local wine merchant.

the style

It's important to think about space, so there is room for people to wander and mingle – choose a large room and move the furniture to the edges. I love serving different drinks, so use an assortment of glasses – it adds glamour, too. Decorate the table with leaves, herbs, strips of fabric and ribbons. Have a few trays handy – you can load one side with nibbles and collect glasses on the other side as you move around the room.

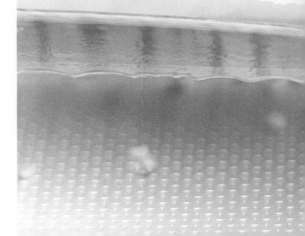

250 g puff pastry

100 g soft, rindless goats' cheese, crumbled

2 cans smoked oysters, 85 g each

1 egg, beaten

sea salt and freshly ground black pepper

a baking sheet, buttered

serves 12

smoked oyster and goats' cheese pastries

I love smoked oysters and I don't think that enough people know about them, so make these little pastries and let everyone enjoy.

Roll out the pastry on a lightly floured surface until very thin, to make a rectangle, then cut in half lengthways. Put half the crumbled goats' cheese down the middle of one piece of pastry. Arrange half the oysters in a row on top of the goats' cheese. Brush the beaten egg along both the long sides, fold the pastry over lengthways and gently press the edges together to seal. Repeat with the other piece of pastry and remaining cheese and oysters. Lightly brush both pastry parcels with beaten egg and then sprinkle with salt and pepper. Cut both into 3 cm slices, transfer to the prepared baking sheet and cook in a preheated oven at 200°C (400°F) Gas 6 for 12 minutes until puffed and golden. Let cool to room temperature before serving.

grissini sticks
with parma ham

It's best to shop for these ingredients at an Italian delicatessen, as the grissini sticks will be skinny and crunchy, made with good flour in the traditional way, and the Parma ham can be sliced to order. Assemble these up to an hour in advance.

12 very thin slices Parma ham

12 grissini (Italian breadsticks)

serves 12

Trim off excess fat from the Parma ham, wrap a slice around each grissini to half the way down, arrange in glasses or on a large plate and serve.

THE WORK PLAN

the day before

- Make the Parmesan and rosemary wafers.

on the day

- Make the smoked oyster and goats' cheese pastries.
- Make the artichoke and bread puffs, but only cook for about 8–10 minutes (finish in oven for 5 minutes just before serving).
- Prepare all the fillings for the ricepaper parcels, put into plastic bags with damp kitchen paper and chill in the refrigerator.

just before serving

- Assemble the ricepaper parcels, arrange on serving dishes.
- Wrap the ham around the grissini and arrange in a glass.
- Chop the raw vegetables and arrange on plates.
- Prepare all the cocktails.

parmesan and
rosemary wafers

These are a must for any good party, as the crispness of the cheese is wonderful and the infusion of the rosemary divine. Everyone will be constantly nibbling, so make lots. They can be prepared in advance but must be kept chilled in an airtight container.

2 sprigs of rosemary, leaves stripped and finely chopped

200 g Parmesan cheese, coarsely grated

2 baking sheets, lined with bakewell paper

makes 24

Put the rosemary into a bowl and stir in the Parmesan. Put teaspoons of the mixture in little heaps on the baking sheets and flatten out into circles, making sure that they are not too close, as they will spread. Bake in a preheated oven at 200°C (400°F) Gas 6 for 8–10 minutes until golden, remove and let cool. Gently peel off the paper and serve.

artichoke and tomato bread puffs

Most supermarkets sell cardboard tubes of croissant or
bread dough: both of these work well. Again, enlist some
help to put these together, as many hands make light work!

300 g ready-made bread dough (*petit pain*)	125 g buffalo mozzarella, cut into 48 pieces	sea salt and freshly ground black pepper
280 g baby artichoke hearts in olive oil	24 cherry tomatoes, halved	*2 baking sheets, buttered*
	6 spring onions, each cut into 8	serves 12

Divide the bread dough into 4, then each again into 12, making 48.
Roll out each piece or flatten with the palm of your hand into a disc.
Transfer to the baking sheets. Drain the artichokes, reserving the oil,
and chop to make 48 pieces. Arrange a piece of artichoke and one
of each of the remaining ingredients on top of each piece of dough,
pushing them lightly into the dough to secure them. Sprinkle with a
little of the reserved artichoke oil and salt and pepper. Cook in a
preheated oven at 180°C (350°F) Gas 4 for 12–15 minutes until
golden and cooked. Serve hot, warm or at room temperature.

raw vegetable platter

8 carrots, cut into batons	2 bunches of radishes, trimmed
8 baby fennel bulbs, trimmed and halved	8 tablespoons extra virgin olive oil
1 cucumber, cut into batons	3 tablespoons balsamic vinegar
	serves 12

Arrange the raw vegetables on a big serving plate.
Mix the oil and vinegar in a small dipping bowl and
serve with the vegetables.

cocktails

white wine fizz

1 bottle white wine, 750 ml

1 litre sparkling mineral water

1 apple, sliced

1 lemon, sliced

1 orange, sliced

1 kiwifruit, sliced

ice cubes

serves 8

Put all the ingredients into a jug, mix and serve.

cosmopolitan

8 shots of vodka,
25 ml each

750 ml cranberry juice

freshly squeezed juice
of 4 limes

ice cubes

serves 8

Put all the ingredients into a
jug and mix. Alternatively,
pour the cranberry juice into
individual glasses and top
with the vodka and lime.

brown cow

1/2 bottle Kahlua, 350 ml

1 litre milk

ice cubes

serves 8

Put all the ingredients into
a jug and mix. Alternatively,
put the Kahlua into
individual glasses, and top
with milk and ice.

luscious and lavish dinner

the scene

Pull out all the stops with this luxury menu. It includes lots of things you've always wanted to make, but never known how – or perhaps even that you could! Well, now is your chance to impress your friends.

the style

Simple and pure, with a magnificent table set with elegant white china to show off the magic of this menu. This is the time to use place cards, and it's definitely the time to enlist an extra pair of hands in the kitchen.

THE MENU

FOR 8 PEOPLE

Smoked Wild Salmon and Scrambled Eggs with Avruga

Watercress Soup

Beef en Croûte

Mustard Sauce

Seasonal Cheese and Green Leaf Salad

Raspberries in Champagne Jelly

TO DRINK

Rosé with the Scrambled Egg

Sauvignon Blanc or Chenin Blanc with the Soup

Cabernet Sauvignon with the Beef and Cheese

Late Harvest Sweet Wine with the Jelly

Reserve Brandy and Coffee

THE WORK PLAN

the day before

- Prepare the beef, wrap it in pastry, cover and chill.
- Make the mustard sauce and chill.

on the day

- Make the champagne jelly.
- Wash and dry the salad leaves, put into a plastic bag and chill.
- Remove the cheese from the refrigerator 2 hours in advance, cover with a clean tea towel.

just before serving

- Cook the beef.
- Make the soup.
- Warm the bread and make the scrambled eggs.
- Reheat the mustard sauce and toss the salad.

smoked wild salmon and scrambled eggs with avruga

Use caviar if you are wildly rich – and try the scrambled eggs made with duck eggs. These are available from some delicatessens and farm shops.

Break the eggs into a bowl and whisk lightly. Add the milk and whisk again. Melt the butter in a non-stick saucepan, then add the eggs and salt and pepper to taste. Cook, stirring constantly with a small wooden spoon, for about 5–8 minutes, until softly scrambled. Remove from the heat just before the eggs are done, as they will carry on cooking off the heat.

Warm the bread in a preheated oven at 180°C (350°F) Gas 4 for 10 minutes and put onto serving plates. Spoon the scrambled eggs onto the toast and top with smoked salmon. Add a teaspoon of avruga, if using, and serve at once, topped with a few chives.

8 hen eggs
or 4 duck eggs

100 ml milk

50 g butter

8 slices mixed grain bread

250 g smoked wild salmon

100 g avruga or salmon caviar (optional)

sea salt and white pepper

a bunch of chives, to serve

serves 8

watercress soup

My green passion is watercress. I love the fresh crunch that releases a subtle peppery taste – such a palate cleanser. Buy it in bunches, with long stems, an abundance of flawless dark green leaves and a clean fresh smell. Store in the refrigerator, wrapped in damp newspaper or kitchen paper, for up to 2 days.

Heat the oil in a large saucepan and add the onion, leek and potatoes. Cook for 15 minutes until soft and translucent. Add the flour, mix well, then add the stock and season with salt and pepper. Heat to simmering and cook for 30 minutes. Using a hand-held stick blender, process until smooth. Add the watercress and parsley and simmer for 5 minutes. Season to taste with salt and pepper, then serve.

2 tablespoons olive oil

1 onion, chopped

1 leek, chopped

2 large potatoes, chopped

2 teaspoons plain flour

1.2 litres chicken or vegetable stock

300 g watercress, stalks removed and leaves chopped

a bunch of flat leaf parsley, chopped

sea salt and freshly ground black pepper

serves 8

4 tablespoons olive oil

3 shallots, finely chopped

2 garlic cloves, chopped

150 g portobello
mushrooms, sliced

1.25 kg fillet of beef,
trimmed

500 g puff or shortcrust
pastry

2 eggs, beaten

sea salt and freshly ground
black pepper

serves 8

beef en croûte

For added luxury, use a mixture of porcini and portobello mushrooms. Just make sure they are completely cold when you put them onto the pastry, and drain off any excess liquid.

Put 2 tablespoons of the oil into a frying pan, heat gently, then add the shallots, garlic and mushrooms. Cook for 15 minutes, stirring frequently, until soft but not browned and all the liquid has evaporated. Season with salt and pepper, let cool, then chill.

Put 1 tablespoon of the remaining oil into a roasting tin and put into a preheated oven at 220°C (425°F) Gas 7 for 5 minutes. Rub the beef fillet all over with the remaining oil and salt and pepper, and transfer to the preheated roasting tin. Cook for 15 minutes, then remove. Transfer the fillet to a plate, reserving the meat juices for the mustard sauce, and let cool until completely cold. (At this stage, you can make the mustard sauce in the roasting tin and reheat it when you need it.)

Roll out the pastry to a rectangle large enough to wrap around the fillet. Brush lightly with the beaten eggs. Spoon the mushroom mixture evenly over the pastry, leaving a 5 cm border all around. Put the cold beef fillet in the middle of the pastry, on top of the mushrooms, and either roll the pastry around the fillet or wrap, as if covering a parcel. Try not to have too much pastry at the ends, and trim to avoid areas of double pastry. Turn the parcel so that the seam is underneath, and transfer to a lightly oiled baking sheet. Brush all over with the beaten eggs and chill for 2 hours.

Cook on the middle shelf of a preheated oven at 200°C (400°F) Gas 6 for 20 minutes. Reduce the oven heat to 180°C (350°F) Gas 4 and continue cooking for 15 minutes for rare, 35 minutes for medium and 50 minutes for well done. If you are cooking to well done, you may need to reduce the oven temperature to prevent the pastry from burning while the beef cooks through.

mustard sauce

This sauce is rather delicious but also rich, so a little goes a long way.

2 tablespoons smooth
Dijon mustard

2 tablespoons wholegrain
mustard

100 ml white wine

400 ml double cream

reserved juices from
roasting the beef fillet

serves 8

Put the mustards, white wine, double cream and roasting juices into a saucepan (if not making in the roasting tin, see above). Bring to the boil, then simmer for 5 minutes. If you are making it in advance, after roasting the fillet, make it in the roasting tin. Serve hot with the beef.

seasonal cheese and green leaf salad

My favourite cheese is Vacherin – if ever a cheese was made in heaven, this is it. It comes from Switzerland and the best time to buy is October–November when the milk used to make the cheese has come from cows fed on spring–summer meadow grass. If you store cheese in the refrigerator, always remove it to room temperature 2 hours before serving.

200 g mizuna or other small salad leaves

200 g rocket

1 head of escarole (Batavia lettuce), leaves separated

2 tablespoons smooth Dijon mustard

75 ml red wine vinegar

200 ml olive oil

1–2 cheeses, depending on variety and size

sea salt and freshly ground black pepper

bread or cheese biscuits, to serve

serves 8

Wash the mizuna, rocket and escarole in a large sink of cold water. Use a salad spinner to dry all the leaves. Put the mustard and vinegar into a large jar with a secure lid and shake well. Add the olive oil, with salt and pepper to taste, and shake vigorously. Transfer the dry lettuce to a large salad bowl and, just before serving, add the dressing. Toss well to coat. Serve the salad with the cheese and bread or biscuits.

raspberries in champagne jelly

This simple but delicious combination is a refreshingly light way to round off an otherwise quite rich menu. If champagne seems a bit decadent, use a good bottle of cava or one of the New World sparkling wines.

25 g gelatine

500 g raspberries

1 bottle champagne, at room temperature

8 glasses

serves 8

Put 3 tablespoons hot water into a small bowl and sprinkle in the gelatine. Set aside in a warm place to dissolve, about 10 minutes. Divide the raspberries between the glasses. Open the champagne and add a little to the dissolved gelatine. Transfer to a jug and add the remaining champagne. Mix gently so that you don't build up a froth. Pour into the glasses on top of the raspberries and chill for 2 hours, until set.

the scene

This menu makes a welcome change after all that traditional Christmas food. The seafood lasagne is light and elegant, but also luxurious, and can be made in advance and reheated.

the style

Cover the table with rich colours and have plenty of candles to match the Christmas tree lights. Wrap a little gift for every guest, to carry on the tradition and spirit of giving into the New Year.

THE MENU

FOR 12 PEOPLE

Beetroot, Goats' Cheese and Pine Nut Salad with Melba Toast

Seafood Lasagne

Dry-fry Chilli Greens

Raspberry and Chocolate Tart

TO DRINK

Gamay with the Salad

Sauvignon Blanc or Chenin Blanc with the Lasagne

Muscat or Sauternes with the Tart

new year's eve dinner

THE WORK PLAN

the day before

- Make the seafood lasagne, cover and chill.
- Make and cook chocolate base for the tart.

on the day

- Make the Melba toast. Store in an airtight container.
- Roast the beetroot, cool and peel.
- Make the salad dressing.
- Prepare the greens.
- Assemble the chocolate tart and freeze. (Remove from freezer 30 minutes before serving.)

just before serving

- Reheat the lasagne in a preheated oven at 180°C (350°F) Gas 4 for 30 minutes, reduce to 150°C (300°F) Gas 2 and cook for 30 minutes.
- Assemble the salad.
- Dress the salad.
- Cook the greens.

beetroot, goats' cheese and pine nut salad with melba toast

Wintry, festive sumptuousness, thanks to the deep red of the beetroot and the bright white of the cheese.

12 slices white, sliced bread

750 g small, unpeeled beetroot, trimmed

500 g mixed leaves

200 g crumbly goats' cheese

100 g pine nuts, toasted in a dry frying pan

a bunch of basil

2 garlic cloves, crushed and chopped

5 tablespoons olive oil

freshly squeezed juice of 2 lemons

salt and freshly ground black pepper

serves 12

To make the Melba toast, toast the slices of bread, then remove the crusts. Using a large, sharp knife, split each piece of toast through the middle, to give 2 whole slices of toast with 1 soft bread side each. Cut in half diagonally, then cook under a preheated grill, soft side up, until golden and curled. Watch the toasts carefully, as they can burn quickly.

Put the beetroot into a roasting tin and roast in a preheated oven at 180°C (350°F) Gas 4 for 45 minutes. Remove, let cool, then peel and quarter. Put the mixed leaves onto a big serving dish, add the beetroot, crumble the goats' cheese on top, then sprinkle with pine nuts and torn basil leaves.

Put the garlic, oil and lemon juice into a small bowl or jar. Add salt and pepper, mix well, then pour over the salad, and serve with the Melba toast.

seafood lasagne

This dish can be prepared completely in advance, leaving you free to enjoy yourself – yet it is still special enough to serve on a big occasion. Choose from prawns, mussels, oysters, crab, lobster, clams, salmon, trout, cod, haddock, tuna, marlin, swordfish, prawns, scallops and skate or other fish. Have a mixture of just four of these fish or seafood and savour the individual flavours. Choose according to your budget and availability and ask your fishmonger for his advice. Anything in a shell, such as mussels or clams, should be removed from the shell and all large pieces of fish should be skinned, boned and cut into even pieces. Make sure you dry all the fish and seafood thoroughly with kitchen paper.

4 tablespoons olive oil

200 g butter

2 garlic cloves, chopped

1 onion, chopped

1 fennel bulb, trimmed and chopped

2 leeks, sliced

100 g plain flour

300 ml fish stock

500 ml white wine

1 kg mixed seafood (see recipe introduction), rinsed and dried

a large bunch of flat leaf parsley, finely chopped

175 ml double cream

500 g dried lasagne

200 g Parmesan cheese, freshly grated

sea salt and freshly ground black pepper

a lasagne or roasting dish, about 30 x 20 cm

serves 12

Put the oil and 50 g of the butter into a large saucepan and heat well. Add the garlic, onion, fennel and leeks and cook for 10 minutes, stirring frequently, until soft and translucent. Using a sieve or flour shaker, sprinkle 25 g of the flour in a thin layer over the top. Mix with a wooden spoon to absorb the excess oil and cook for a few minutes. Gradually add the fish stock and 100 ml of the wine, stirring constantly to form a smooth sauce.

Add the prepared seafood and parsley to the sauce with salt and pepper to taste. Gently mix and simmer over low heat for 5 minutes. Remove from the heat and set aside.

Heat the remaining butter in another saucepan, add the remaining flour and stir until smooth. Cook for a few minutes, then remove from the heat and slowly add the remaining wine, stirring with a balloon whisk. When all the wine has been added, return the saucepan to the heat, bring to the boil and simmer for 2 minutes. Add the cream, salt and pepper, then remove from the heat.

Put a layer of the prepared seafood into the lasagne dish, pour over some sauce and top with a layer of lasagne. Repeat until the dish is full and all the seafood, sauce and lasagne have been used. Top with the Parmesan and chill until needed.

Bake the lasagne in a preheated oven at 180°C (350°F) Gas 4 for 50 minutes until bubbling and golden.

dry-fry chilli greens

I know this is a last minute dish, but really it is so easy that it won't put you under pressure and the result is just delicious, especially with the seafood lasagne. For the greens, use a selection of curly kale, cavolo nero, Savoy cabbage or red chard.

1 tablespoon
vegetable oil

25 g butter

500 g greens,
coarsely chopped

½ teaspoon
crushed dried
red chillies

zest and juice
of 2 unwaxed
lemons

freshly ground
black pepper

serves 12

Heat the oil and butter in a wok or large saucepan, add the greens and cook for 5 minutes, tossing frequently. Add the dried chillies, lemon zest and juice. Cook for a further minute and transfer to a serving dish. Sprinkle with pepper and serve.

raspberry and chocolate tart

200 g butter

200 g dark chocolate (70 per cent cocoa solids), broken into pieces

4 eggs

200 g unrefined caster sugar

200 g self-raising flour

100 g ground almonds

375 g raspberries

500 g raspberry yoghurt ice cream

a springform cake tin, 24 cm diameter, buttered

serves 12

Put the butter and chocolate into a saucepan and melt gently over very low heat. Put the eggs and sugar into a bowl and whisk, using an electric beater, for 6 minutes until stiff and creamy. Pour the melted chocolate into the eggs and sugar and continue whisking until mixed. Using a large metal spoon, fold in the flour and ground almonds. Pour the mixture into the prepared cake tin and top with about one third of the raspberries.

Bake in a preheated oven at 180°C (350°F) Gas 4 for 30–40 minutes until set, then remove and let cool in the tin. When cool, turn out the cake onto a plate. Pile the ice cream on top, then push the remaining raspberries into the ice cream. Transfer to the freezer for up to 2 hours, but remove 20 minutes before serving.

index